KT-473-308

EXPERIMENTAL DESIGN IN EDUCATION

EXPERIMENTAL DESIGN IN EDUCATION

D. G. Lewis

UNIVERSITY OF LONDON PRESS LTD

SBN 340 07342 X

University of London Press Ltd
St Paul's House, Warwick Lane, London EC4

Printed in Great Britain by
Alden & Mowbray Ltd
at the Alden Press, Oxford
and bound at the Kemp Hall Bindery

Contents

List of Figures

List of Tables

List of Statistical Tables

Preface

This book provides an account of the ideas underlying the design of experiments in education. The need for such a book is evident from the increasing attention now being given to educational research, and the consequent necessity to provide further training for teachers and social workers in the techniques of experimentation. A related consideration is that up to the present almost all the books on experimental design base their accounts on illustrations from the fields of industry, agriculture or medicine. It is hoped, therefore, that the present book, written largely—though not exclusively—for the research worker in education, will serve a real need.

An attempt has been made to develop the subject without assuming very much prior knowledge of statistics. Thus, in chapter 1 the reader is introduced to such basic concepts as statistical error, randomization, hypothesis-testing and estimation. Many readers, however, might prefer to come to grips with this discussion only after having read a basic text on statistical methods, such as the writer's *Statistical Methods in Education.* The general plan has been to explain the purpose of a particular design, then the method of computation, and then the theoretical model on which it is based. A knowledge of elementary algebra, or at least of algebraic symbolism, is necessary if the exposition of the models is to be followed in full; yet it is hoped that even those averse to mathematical expression may follow the main themes of the book.

The designs chosen are the ones most frequently applied in educational research. They include those of randomized groups, randomized blocks, the covariance design and the factorial design, with its modifications to allow for the nesting as well as the crossing of variables. All assume measurement on an ordinal or interval scale, and so permit an analysis of variance. Detailed attention has been given throughout the book to the calculation of sums of squares and degrees of freedom, since the student wishing to apply these procedures to his own data will need firm assurance here. References for further study are given at the end of the chapters.

I am grateful to Professor F. W. Warburton of the University of Manchester for reading the manuscript and for making many helpful suggestions. Thanks are also due to the publisher's readers for their comments. I am, of course, solely responsible for any defects that remain. Finally I must record my thanks to Miss Mary Flint of University of London Press Ltd for the efficiency and courtesy with which she has dealt with all matters leading to the publication of this book.

D. G. Lewis
June 1967

'Statistical procedure and experimental design are only two aspects of the same whole, and that whole comprises all the logical requirements of the complete process of adding to natural knowledge by experimentation.'

Ronald A. Fisher, *The Design of Experiments*

Chapter 1 Basic Concepts

1.1 The recognition of statistical error

It is nowadays commonplace to recognize the contribution of statistics to experiment in education and the social sciences. Investigators, including those still learning the techniques of research by writing theses for higher degrees, are aware that their results must be assessed statistically. They realize that findings obtained from relatively small numbers of subjects, the sample, have to be generalized, if at all possible, to include the larger numbers with respect to which the sample may be considered a representative part. Statisticians are therefore consulted to aid in formulating the conclusions that may properly be drawn from the experiment.

There is, however, a noticeably smaller degree of awareness that the help of statisticians could well be sought *before* the experiment is conducted, that statistical principles should in fact govern the actual planning of the experiment. A failure to realize this could well lead to disappointment, in that the data might have been obtained in a way that diminished, if not virtually excluded, the possibility of a particular hypothesis being verified. Of course, such verification could never be absolute. A margin of 'error'—statistical error—is necessarily present, however skilfully the experiment is designed. But with an unplanned, or haphazardly planned, experiment this margin of error could well be, and probably would be, unnecessarily large.

Statistical error in the social sciences may be viewed as a result of the perversity of human nature: human beings invariably differ from each other in all manner of ways. Experimental results will vary in different experiments, even when these experiments are repetitions of the same basic one and are all conducted in a similar manner but with different samples of subjects. They would also vary if the same subjects were tested on a second occasion. Allowance for this—the fundamental fact of individual differences—needs to be built in to every experimental design.

As an illustration, consider the two sets of eight scores shown in table 1.1. They are, we will suppose, the scores of eight arts and eight science students on a test of creativity, a test which probes the creative aspects of one's thinking, such as the ability to formulate an answer to an unexpected question rather than to select an answer from a number of given alternatives. Considerable variation in the scores is apparent, though many psychologists might comment that as an illustration of the data they work with the scores in table 1.1 are remarkably uniform. The purpose of the investigation would be to compare the creativity of arts and science students.

Table 1.1 Scores of eight arts and eight science students on a creativity test

	Arts	*Science*
	63	58
	61	56
	58	56
	57	54
	55	51
	52	50
	52	48
	50	47
Total score	448	420
Mean score	56·0	52·5

Our interest, of course, is not in the scores themselves. Each of the eight arts students' scores is of interest only in so far as it represents the test performance of arts students generally; and the same is true for the eight science students' scores. Obviously, then, it is the mean score of each of the groups which merit our attention in the first place. Further, the dispersion of scores within each of the two groups are instances of statistical error.

An additional point is that statistical error necessarily affects the value of the mean scores themselves. If, in other words, the experiment were repeated with different students, different mean scores would almost certainly result. How, then, can we be sure that the present difference in mean score, and, in particular, the *direction* of the difference—which indicates that arts students generally are more creative in their thinking than science students—is reliable? To obtain an answer to this question, statisticians consider the experiment to be just one of a series of similar experiments, experiments identical in design and implementation, but with different subjects. With a long series of such experiments, the differences in mean score could be expected to cluster round some fixed value. This value—which would in fact be the mean of the series of differences in mean score—is termed the *true difference*. The problem then becomes one of generalization. Knowing only the one obtained difference, what can be inferred about the true difference?

1.2 Hypothesis-testing

One approach to the problem of generalization consists of formulating, and then attempting to disprove, a *null hypothesis*. A null hypothesis states that there is no true difference between the measures being sampled, so that any obtained difference is due to chance, i.e. to the fluctuations of sampling.* It follows that, for the data of table 1.1, the difference in means of 3·5 must be viewed as one of a series of possible differences—obtained from repetitions, or *replications* as they are termed, of the same basic experiment—the distribution of these differences being centred at zero. Statistical techniques have been developed giving the frequency with which differences at least as great as the obtained difference would then arise. (The frequency with which the difference of 3·5 in table 1.1 would arise is evaluated later, pp. 29–30.) If this frequency is sufficiently small—and the interpretation of 'sufficiently' is left to the investigator—the null hypothesis is rejected, and a true difference accepted.

A common practice has been to accept a true difference only if the frequency, expressed as a percentage of the total frequency, does not exceed 5 per cent, or alternatively 1 per cent. These criteria provide the 5-per-cent

* More generally, a null hypothesis must be an exact hypothesis. Thus it could state the true difference to be any fixed amount, though in practice this amount is almost always taken as zero. On the other hand, the alternative to the null hypothesis as stated above, namely that the difference is some (unspecified) non-zero amount, is not eligible as a null hypothesis because it is not exact.

and 1-per-cent *levels of significance*. They are, however, of only conventional importance, and an investigator is free to adopt other levels if he wishes. Two conflicting aims are involved. One is to reduce the likelihood of a null hypothesis being rejected when it is true, an aim which is achieved by lowering the frequency. This, however, renders more difficult the realization of the second aim, that of not accepting a null hypothesis too often when it is false. A balance between these two aims must be struck in the light of the practical considerations involved. Thus, if the acceptance of a true difference was likely to involve sweeping changes in educational practice, with the expenditure of a large sum of money, the reduction in the likelihood of a true hypothesis being rejected becomes the more important consideration. A rejection of a null hypothesis which happens to be true is termed an *error of type 1*, while an acceptance of a null hypothesis which happens to be false is termed an *error of type 2*.

We need to consider, too, the alternative which would be accepted if the null hypothesis were rejected. In the present illustration, the alternative is clearly that *some* difference (direction unspecified) exists between the creativity of thinking of arts and science students; the level of significance would therefore have to be decided by a two-tailed test. If, for example, the obtained difference of 3·5 in table 1.1 were found to be significant at the 10-per-cent level, it would mean that differences of 3·5 or more in favour of the arts students would be found in replications of the experiment 5 per cent of the time, and similar differences in favour of the science students a further 5 per cent of the time. Occasionally, however, differences in one direction only are expected—or, at any rate, any differences found in the unexpected direction would necessarily be due to chance. If, for instance, the same students sat the same, or a parallel, test on a second occasion—the purpose of the experiment being to gauge practice effect—a true difference could only be such as to increase the score on the second occasion. In such a case, the alternative to the null hypothesis would be some difference in one (specified) direction, and a one-tailed test of significance would be appropriate.

1.3 Estimation

The main benefit from tests of significance is the caution they induce. Investigators might otherwise be tempted into extravagant claims. At the same time the practical usefulness of these tests is limited. Often, too, they cannot but seem artificial, in that for many experiments some true difference is almost inevitable. The more important question would be whether the difference is great enough to justify action. An estimate of the true difference is usually a more worth-while goal.

The procedure is one which results in two limits within which the true difference will probably lie, the degree of probability being precisely determined. The degree of probability in fact is decided on first. For instance, with an 80-per-cent degree of probability the calculation would result in limits which have an 80-per-cent chance (four chances out of five) of including the true difference between them. For the data of table 1.1 such limits would be 0·58 and 6·42 in favour of the arts students. If an 80-per-cent probability is considered too low, a higher probability could be decided on—but naturally at the expense of widening the limits. With a 95-per-cent probability the limits, from the data of table 1.1, become $-1{\cdot}15$ and 8·15, i.e. 1·15 in favour of the science students and 8·15 in favour of the arts students; and with a 99-per-cent probability the limits are $-2{\cdot}96$ and 9·96. The limits are called *confidence limits*, those for the 95-per-cent and 99-per-cent probabilities being the ones most often used. The result is always an assertion that the true difference lies between the calculated limits, together with a statement of the probability that this assertion is correct.

The only practical outcome of the determination of confidence limits for the data of table 1.1 is that the data are indecisive. No firm decision that arts students generally have a greater creativity of thinking can be made, though there is some indication that this may be so.* The numbers of students (eight in each group) are too small—a conclusion that would have been expected by anyone familiar with data of this type. If, on the other hand, the 95-per-cent confidence limits had been, say, 2·00 and 4·50, the decision as to the greater creativity of thinking in arts students could reasonably be made. We could still, however, question the psychological, as distinct from the statistical, significance of the result. A difference even of 4·5 points of score might be too small on which to base, say, recommendations for a change in the teaching of science students, or for a change in their syllabuses of study for 'minority time'.

* With widely separated limits roughly centred about zero, on the other hand, no indication of any kind is provided, not even that the two populations do not differ in the attribute tested.

1.4 Randomization

In our illustration of statistical error, test scores from the two groups of students were compared. We did not, however, define precisely what we were discussing. We really need to know who are the arts and science students whose creativity scores we are comparing. Are they, for instance, university graduates (and, if so, with honours degrees, or pass degrees, or either), undergraduates, or grammar-school sixth-formers; are they male or female, or both; are they selected from the whole country or just from one area (e.g. the Home Counties), or from one Local Education Authority, or even from one school? Obviously we need to define the *population* of students—or rather the two populations of students (one arts, one science) —we wish to compare.

To fix our ideas, we will suppose that the two populations in which we are interested are those of grammar-school sixth-formers specializing in arts and science, and that we are confining our attention, initially at any rate, to one school. It is imperative, then, that we select *random samples* of arts and science sixth-formers from that school. (The test scores set out in table 1.1, in fact—if the previous discussion is not to be invalidated from the outset—must be the scores obtained by such samples.) A random sample is one in which every member of the population has an equal chance of being selected. This implies that no choice is left to the investigator: he cannot decide that any particular member must be included (or excluded). It also implies that the selection of any particular member in no way influences the chances of selection of another. The population, in fact, can best be defined as the aggregate or totality in which every member has an equal, and a known, chance of being selected in the sample. Generally the most satisfactory way of ensuring a random sample is to use *tables of random numbers*, such as those of Kendall and Babington Smith (1939), Fisher and Yates (1963), or Snedecor (1956).

It may often be impractical to sample by direct randomization. This is usually so when the population is very large, and when it would therefore be very time-consuming to number each member, a necessary preliminary to the use of random number tables. In this case a *stratified random sample* is selected. The population is initially separated into strata on the basis of some clearly defined feature or 'control', and a random sample is selected within each stratum. The size of each of these samples, too, could be made proportional to the size of the stratum. The control determining the strata is usually such that a considerable variation could be expected between the strata, the population being more homogeneous (with respect to the characteristic under investigation) within each of the strata. For an investigation on the creativity of thinking of sixth-formers, for example, the size of the sixth form, with its consequent influence on the educational facilities provided, might be considered an effective control. A stratified sample of sixth-formers could then be selected on the basis of sixth-form size, categories of pupils in, say, large, medium and small sixth forms being formed, and random subsamples then being selected within each category of size. A further point is that it may prove unduly troublesome to select random samples of *pupils*, as the sample would be spread out over a large number of schools (with possibly only one or two pupils in several of the schools). A more practical procedure would then be to select in the first place random samples of schools.

Despite these and other possible complications, randomization at some stage is an essential ingredient in every experimental design. One reason is that it usually produces a reasonably representative sample, and, in particular, it avoids bias. In our arts–science illustration, for instance, it would obviously be wrong to select only the most able arts students if a similar restriction were not made for those studying science. Exact equalization is rarely achieved, however. In any particular sample pair the arts students might still be, on average, more able. This, however, would be due to chance alone, and would be allowed for in tests of significance and in the estimations of a true difference. This brings us to the second reason for randomness, namely that it permits the element of chance to operate in a way that can be rigorously assessed. These, and other related considerations, are developed more fully in an account by Cox (1958).

Randomness, as we have seen, may be achieved in more than one way. Suppose, to develop the present illustration one stage further, that a sex difference in creativity of thinking has been suggested from previous research. It would then be sensible to select separately random groups of boys and girls (for example, four boys and four girls for each of the arts and science groups) rather than random groups of eight for boys and girls combined. It is true, of course, that selecting random groups of eight in this way *could* by chance produce groups of four boys and four girls. But if equal numbers of boys and girls were deliberately selected, the true difference between the arts and science students would have to be estimated in a different way. (The procedure would be that of a randomized-blocks design described in chapter 5, not that of a randomized-groups design described in chapter 3.) A valid determination of confidence limits (for the arts–science difference) is possible in both designs, and when the sexes are selected separately, confidence limits for the difference between sexes could also be obtained. This brings out the point that the design of an experiment determines not only what kinds of conclusions are possible, but also the mode of analysis necessary to arrive at them. Considerations of design are basic to all else.

1.5 The key role of design

Statistical error in the field of education is usually very considerable, as human material is so intrinsically variable, and, in fact, many investigations would be doomed to inconclusiveness unless very large numbers of subjects were used (a possibility often precluded by the limitations of time, labour and financial support), or else the investigation were designed in such a way as to reduce the error to manageable proportions. Even if a superabundance of resources were available, it would still, of course, be wasteful to proceed with an inefficient design. This key role of design—that of reducing statistical error and so rendering the experiment more sensitive —may be seen in an illustration adapted from one first formulated by Fisher in his *The Design of Experiments* (1951), and which has since become classical.

A person claims to be able to detect a difference in flavour in a cup of tea according to whether the tea or the milk is poured in first. The following experiment is suggested to investigate the claim. Four cups of tea are prepared, three with the milk poured in first and one with the tea poured in first, all four drinks being otherwise as near identical as practicable (for example, all are at the same temperature, all have exactly the same amount of milk, and all the cups are of the same size and material and have the same pattern). The person making the claim has the four cups of tea presented to him in random order, and he has to detect which one has been prepared differently from the rest. The null hypothesis is that no difference in flavour can be detected. On this basis, the cup of tea selected as different would be the differently prepared cup only as often as could be expected from chance. A single trial is of limited value, so a series of trials is proposed, a separate set of four cups of tea being prepared for each trial.

The possible results, together with their probability of occurrence on the basis of the null hypothesis, can then be readily specified.

Suppose that the complete experiment consists of five trials. For each trial the probability of the correct cup being chosen is 1/4. With five trials the possible results, with their probabilities will be as follows.*

None correct	$\frac{243}{1024}$	3 correct	$\frac{90}{1024}$
1 correct	$\frac{405}{1024}$	4 correct	$\frac{15}{1024}$
2 correct	$\frac{270}{1024}$	5 correct	$\frac{1}{1024}$

If, therefore, the person achieves success in all five trials, the evidence against the null hypothesis is very strong, since such a result would be expected from chance only once in 1024 similar experiments—a probability of $\frac{1}{1024}$ or less than 0·1 per cent. If, however, the person makes one mistake, and succeeds in four of the five trials, the probability of this, together with that of the one better result, occurring by chance is $\frac{16}{1024}$ = 1·56 per cent; so the null hypothesis could no longer be rejected, and the result accepted as significant, at the 1-per-cent level. Again, if the person makes two mistakes, choosing the correct cup in only two of the trials, the probability of this, together with that of the two better results, is $\frac{106}{1024}$ = 10·35 per cent. The null hypothesis would not then be rejected even at the 10-per-cent level.

The possibility of mistakes should be considered, since the person might not claim infallibility: if he were to claim this, a single mistake would, of course, be decisive. His claim might be that he can correctly detect the differently prepared cup of tea more often than could be attributed to chance. He might even quantify his claim by saying that he could, on average, detect the 'odd' cup once in every two trials, i.e. a probability of 1/2 as against a chance probability of only 1/4. On this basis, therefore, the probabilities of the five possible results will be as follows:†

* The probabilities may be deduced from the binomial expansion. If p is the probability of a single correct result, and $q = (1-p)$ is the probability of this result *not* being obtained, then with a set of n trials the probability of 0, 1, 2, ... correct results being obtained is given by the successive terms of the binomial expansion $(q+p)^n$. In the present experiment $p = \frac{1}{4}$, $q = \frac{3}{4}$ and $n = 5$.

† With the notation of the footnote above, $p = \frac{1}{2}$, $q = \frac{1}{2}$ and $n = 5$.

None correct	$\frac{1}{32}$	3 correct	$\frac{10}{32}$
1 correct	$\frac{5}{32}$	4 correct	$\frac{5}{32}$
2 correct	$\frac{10}{32}$	5 correct	$\frac{1}{32}$

If we had decided, when testing the null hypothesis, to adopt a 5-per-cent level of significance—so that either four or five correct results would be accepted as evidence of the person's ability to detect a difference in taste—we see that the probability of getting this evidence is now only $\frac{6}{32} = 18{\cdot}75$ per cent. We would, therefore, fail to acknowledge the person's ability to detect a difference in taste very frequently, over 80 per cent of the time. Our conclusion is that the experiment as at present designed is lacking in sensitiveness. It would be better if the experiment were designed so that even if more than one mistake were made (i.e. less than four correct results being obtained), the null hypothesis could be rejected at, say, the 5-per-cent level.

In general, the sensitiveness of an experiment can be increased in three ways. These are:

1. Increasing the size of the experiment.
2. Refining the experimental techniques.
3. Altering the experiment's internal structure, i.e. improving the design.

The size of the present experiment would be increased simply by adding on more trials. Thus, the reader may care to verify that with six trials instead of five, the probability of one or no mistakes would fall to 0·46 per cent, so that the null hypothesis would then be rejected at the 1-per-cent level. And if two mistakes were made, the probability (of this together with that of the two better results) would be 3·76 per cent, so that the null hypothesis would then be rejected at the 5-per-cent level.

Refining the experimental techniques consists of removing extraneous influences which, in the present experiment, would have the effect of confusing the drinker and impairing any ability he may have in detecting the claimed difference in taste. Some possible influences have been mentioned. Thus, if the cups of tea were at different temperatures, it might interfere with the detection of differences in taste. Similarly, the kind of tea used should be the same throughout the experiment. So, too, should the strength of the tea, the kind of milk used and the amount of sugar added. But it is well to bear in mind that the process of refining the experimental techniques is without limit. However careful the investigator has been, an additional precaution (an ingenious one possibly, involving extra labour and expense) can always be proposed. There comes a point when it is more sensible to proceed. What is important, however, is that an extraneous influence which has not been controlled—i.e. equalized among the experimental material—should, if possible, be randomized. (Thus, while it would be easy to arrange for all the tea to be of the same kind, it would not be so easy to equalize the strength of the brew. But if in any one trial the five cups are poured from the same pot, the one with the tea poured in before the milk should not be the first cup from the pot in every trial. Rather the order of the cup chosen for the different treatment—the tea poured in first—should be selected randomly, and separately, at each trial.)

The third way of increasing the sensitiveness of an experiment—that of improving its design—may be seen from the fact that in the experiment now under consideration we need not arrange for only one cup of tea out of every four to have been treated differently from the rest. We could have two cups of tea treated in this way, the person claiming to be able to detect a difference in taste being asked to separate these two cups from the other two. In any one trial the probability of the correct two cups being chosen by chance is 1/6.* With five trials as before, the probabilities of the different possible results appear as:

None correct	$\frac{3125}{7776}$	3 correct	$\frac{250}{7776}$
1 correct	$\frac{3125}{7776}$	4 correct	$\frac{25}{7776}$
2 correct	$\frac{1250}{7776}$	5 correct	$\frac{1}{7776}$

A dramatic drop in the probabilities is evident. The chance probability of one or no mistakes is now $\frac{26}{7776} = 0{\cdot}33$ per cent, so that with only one mistake the overall result would be significant at the 1-per-cent level. And with two mistakes the probability (of this and the two better results) is only $\frac{276}{7776} = 3{\cdot}55$ per cent, as against one of over 10 per cent before, so giving an overall result significant at the 5-per-cent level. Clearly this change in design is well worth while. Moreover, the benefit would accrue whatever size of experiment (i.e. number of trials) was decided upon.

* The first cup chosen would be any of the four, and the second any one of the remaining three, making $4 \times 3 = 12$ ways of choosing two cups *in different orders*. As the same pair of cups could themselves be chosen in two orders, the number of ways of choosing two cups without having regard to which is chosen first is 1/2 of 12 = 6.

The changed design makes use of the available resources in a more effective manner.

The most effective use of the experimental material constitutes the key role of design. This is why an investigator—if he is not himself skilled in design—should consult a statistician before, rather than after, the experiment has taken place. Otherwise his experiment may not be sensitive enough to permit definite conclusions to be reached. Sometimes the nature of the problem may suggest that additional measures be taken, the extra trouble and expense being amply repaid by the increased information that will be forthcoming. Often more information can be obtained by grouping the subjects taking part, so that the groups will be more closely alike in certain respects. This grouping, too, may be carried out in more than one way; and possibly more than one set of measures may be taken from the same groups. A description of these possibilities forms the subject matter of this book.

References

COX, D. R. (1958) *Planning of Experiments*, New York: Wiley, pp. 70–90.

FISHER, R. A. (1951) *The Design of Experiments*, Edinburgh: Oliver & Boyd (6th edition), chapter 2.

FISHER, R. A. and YATES, F. (1963) *Statistical Tables for Biological, Agricultural and Medical Research*, Edinburgh: Oliver & Boyd (6th edition), pp. 134–9.

KENDALL, M. G. and BABINGTON SMITH, B. (1939) *Tables of Random Sampling Numbers Tracts for Computers*, **24**, Cambridge: Cambridge University Press.

SNEDECOR, G. W. (1956) *Statistical Methods*, Iowa State College Press (5th edition), pp. 10–13.

Chapter 2 The *t* and *F* Ratios

2.1 The *t* test of significance

A question that frequently occurs in educational research is whether an obtained difference between the mean scores of two groups may be taken as sound evidence of a real, non-chance difference. In tackling this, the sampling variability of each of the two means has to be considered. It has been found that the best way of assessing this sampling variability is through the sum of the squares of the deviations of the scores in each group from their mean.

Let us consider again the test scores of the groups of arts and science students shown in table 1.1. The deviations of these scores from their own group mean (from 56·0 for the scores of the arts students, and from 52·5 for those of the science students) are shown in table 2.1. The sum of squares of the deviations for each group—i.e. $7{\cdot}0^2+5{\cdot}0^2+\cdots+(-6{\cdot}0)^2$ for the arts group, and $5{\cdot}5^2+3{\cdot}5^2+\cdots+(-5{\cdot}5)^2$ for the science group—works out as 148 and 116. These provide, in relation to the size of the group, an estimate of the sampling variability of the scores of arts and science students (of the type sampled) generally. An unbiased estimate of the population variance would, in fact, be provided for each category of students by dividing the sum of squares by the group size minus 1.

The sampling variability of a *mean* score, on the other hand—i.e. the extent to which a mean score can be expected to vary as different samples of the same size are randomly selected from the same population—is most conveniently expressed by its *standard error*. The standard error of any sample measure, such as a mean, is the standard deviation of its sampling distribution, or, more fully, the standard deviation of the distribution of measures that would result if large numbers of different samples of the same size were randomly selected from the same population. With a sample of size n, the standard error of the mean, σ_M, is given by the formula

$$\sigma_M = \frac{\sigma}{\sqrt{n}} \tag{1}$$

σ being the standard deviation of the distribution of individual scores in the population. This formula assumes that the population is large, in theory infinitely large, so that by comparison the size of the sample is negligible.*

Similarly with two mean scores—means from samples selected randomly and independently from two populations—the standard error of the difference between the means $\sigma_{(M_1-M_2)}$ is given by

$$\sigma_{(M_1-M_2)} = \sqrt{\frac{\sigma_1^2}{n_1}+\frac{\sigma_2^2}{n_2}} \qquad (2)$$

σ_1 and σ_2 being the standard deviations of the scores in the two populations, and n_1 and n_2 the two sample sizes.

The practical difficulty in applying this theory is that the population variances are almost always unknown. σ_1^2 and σ_2^2 are parameters which have to be estimated from the available data. We have mentioned that an estimate of a population variance—and one which is unbiased, in that estimates derived in the same way from large numbers of similar samples would be centred around the actual population variance—is obtained by dividing the sum of the squares of the deviations of the scores by the sample size minus 1. Thus, with the suffices 1 and 2 referring to the arts and science groups respectively, an unbiased estimate of σ_1^2 is provided by

$$\hat{\sigma}_1^2 = \frac{148{\cdot}00}{7} = 21{\cdot}14 \qquad \text{(see table 2.1)}$$

and one of σ_2^2 by

$$\hat{\sigma}_2^2 = \frac{116{\cdot}00}{7} = 16{\cdot}57$$

(The circumflex sign is used to show that it is an estimated value of the parameter, and not the parameter itself, which has been obtained.) Often, however, we have no reason to suppose that the two parameters differ, i.e. that σ_1 does not equal σ_2. On this basis we may estimate the common population variance by combining the data from both groups as follows:

* If this were not the case, the formula would appear as $\sigma_M = \frac{\sigma}{\sqrt{n}} \cdot \sqrt{1-\varphi}$, where φ is the *sampling fraction*, i.e. the fraction of the population included in the sample. The factor $\sqrt{1-\varphi}$ would also enter into the other standard error formulae considered in this chapter.

$$\hat{\sigma}^2 = \frac{148{\cdot}00+116{\cdot}00}{7+7} = \frac{264{\cdot}00}{14} = 18{\cdot}86$$

This is the best estimate of the population variance (assumed to be the same for both groups) in that it is based on all the available data. Generally for samples of sizes n_1 and n_2 (not necessarily equal) the denominator for obtaining $\hat{\sigma}^2$ would be $(n_1-1)+(n_2-1)$ or n_1+n_2-2.

Table 2.1 Analysis of the data in table 1.1

	Deviations of scores from their group mean	
	Arts	*Science*
	7·0	5·5
	5·0	3·5
	2·0	3·5
	1·0	1·5
	−1·0	−1·5
	−4·0	−2·5
	−4·0	−4·5
	−6·0	−5·5
Sum of squares	148·00	116·00
Estimate of population variance	$\frac{148{\cdot}00}{7} = 21{\cdot}14$	$\frac{116{\cdot}00}{7} = 16{\cdot}57$
Estimate from both samples	$\frac{148{\cdot}00+116{\cdot}00}{7+7} = \frac{264{\cdot}00}{14} = 18{\cdot}86$	
S.E. of difference between means	$\sqrt{18{\cdot}86\,(\frac{1}{8}+\frac{1}{8})} = 2{\cdot}17$	

The standard error of the difference between two mean scores is now evaluated by replacing both σ_1^2 and σ_2^2 in formula (2) by the best estimate $\hat{\sigma}^2$. The formula then becomes

$$\hat{\sigma}_{(M_1-M_2)} = \sqrt{\hat{\sigma}^2\left(\frac{1}{n_1}+\frac{1}{n_2}\right)} \qquad (3)$$

The circumflex now appears over the symbol $\sigma_{(M_1-M_2)}$ since this formula, unlike formula (2), provides only an estimate of the standard error of the difference between the means. The important point, however, is that this can be evaluated entirely from the test scores themselves. For the arts–science data of table 1.1, the estimated standard error works out as 2·17, as shown at the bottom of table 2.1.

The ratio of an obtained difference in mean scores to the estimated standard error of this difference is known as the *t ratio.** In symbols

$$t = \frac{M_1 - M_2}{\hat{\sigma}_{(M_1-M_2)}} \tag{4}$$

When the scores of each group are random samples from normally distributed populations—and as a consequence the sampling distribution of the difference between the means is also normal—the sampling distribution of the t ratios will follow the distribution defined by

$$y = \frac{\Gamma\left(\frac{\nu+1}{2}\right)}{\sqrt{\nu}\,\Gamma\left(\frac{1}{2}\right)\Gamma\left(\frac{\nu}{2}\right)}\left[1+\frac{t^2}{\nu}\right]^{-\frac{1}{2}(\nu+1)} \tag{5}$$

in which Γ denotes the gamma function as defined in standard tests on theory of functions. This distribution is known as the *t distribution.* We see that it depends not only on t but also on ν, a symbol not as yet defined. ν, however, is the same as n_1+n_2-2, the denominator used in obtaining $\hat{\sigma}^2$, or—as it is usually termed—the number of *degrees of freedom* on which $\hat{\sigma}^2$ is based.† There are therefore many t distributions, one for each value of ν. Figure 1 shows the shape of the distribution when ν is small (10 or less). The normal distribution is also shown for comparison. As the degrees of freedom increase, the t distribution approaches the normal distribution. When $\nu = 30$, in fact, the difference between the two distributions is small.

* More generally the t ratio may be defined as the ratio of any statistic (mean, median, correlation, difference between two correlations, etc.) to an unbiased estimate of its standard error.

† The number of degrees of freedom for a population variance estimated from a single sample is one less than the sample size. For a population variance estimated from two independent samples, the number is the sum of the degrees of freedom for the estimates for the separate samples.

Statistical table 1* shows for different numbers of degrees of freedom the values of t necessary to enclose all except a given percentage of frequencies. Thus, for $\nu = 14$, the degrees of freedom on which the estimated

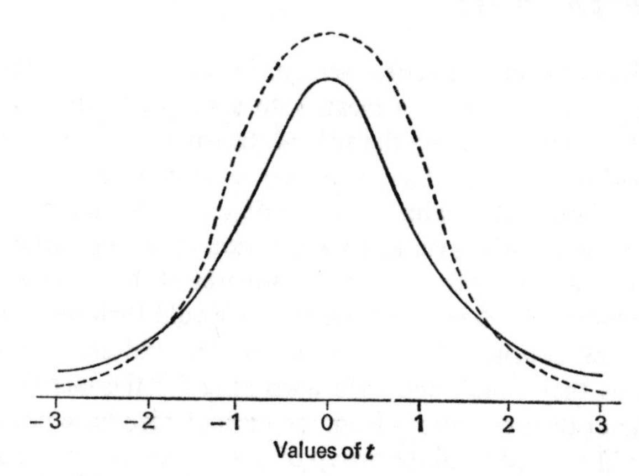

Figure 1 The t distribution for a small number of degrees of freedom, compared with the normal distribution (shown by a broken line).

population variance in table 2.1 is based, a value of 2·145 is necessary for significance at the 5-per-cent level (for a two-tailed test), since values greater than this (in either direction) will occur only 5 per cent of the time. The t ratio resulting from this data is $\frac{56{\cdot}00 - 52{\cdot}50}{2{\cdot}17} = \frac{3{\cdot}50}{2{\cdot}17} = 1{\cdot}61$, which is less than this. It is less even than the value necessary for significance at the 10-per-cent level (1·761). Obviously no reliable evidence for a greater creativity in the thinking of arts students is provided by the data of table 1.1.

Incidentally, the confidence limits described in chapter 1 (p. 17) are determined from the t values for 14 degrees of freedom recorded in statistical table 1. Thus, those for an 80-per-cent degree of probability—i.e. the limits so calculated failing to include the true difference 20 per cent

* Note that the statistical tables are to be distinguished from the tables. The statistical tables are numbered with a single number consecutively through the book; the tables are numbered with a double number by chapter.

of the time—are obtained from the t value in the 20-per-cent column, 1·345, as $3{\cdot}50 \pm 1{\cdot}345 \times 2{\cdot}17 = 3{\cdot}50 \pm 2{\cdot}92 = 0{\cdot}58$ and 6·42.

2.2 The computation of *t*

Of the two groups of test scores set out in table 1.1, one has a whole-number mean and the other a mean with a simple fraction, so that the deviations from the mean and the sum of the squares of the deviations are obtained without trouble. Generally, however, a mean score does not work out to a convenient value, and squaring and summing the deviations might well prove laborious (unless one has access to a calculating machine). A method of calculating the sum of the squares of the deviations without actually obtaining the deviations themselves would then be desirable.

The method consists of summing the scores, and also the squares of the scores, as they stand, and then correcting for the fact that it is the scores, and not their deviations from the mean, which have been summed. This can be illustrated from the group of arts scores from table 1.1 set out again below. The letter x refers to any of the scores, and x^2 to the square of any of the scores. Σ (sigma) is the symbol used to denote summing, so that for Σx we read 'the sum of all the xs (i.e. the scores)', and similarly for Σx^2 we read 'the sum of all the squares of the scores'. The sums Σx and Σx^2 are obtained together with a correction term $\frac{(\Sigma x)^2}{n}$, n being the number of scores in the list (in this case eight). The correction term is then subtracted from Σx^2 to give what is termed the *corrected* sum of squares, a sum which we see to be identical with the sum of squared deviations obtained in table 2.1.

x	x^2
63	3969
61	3721
58	3364
57	3249
55	3025
52	2704
52	2704
50	2500
$\Sigma x = 448$	$\Sigma x^2 = 25{,}236$

Correction term, $\frac{(\Sigma x)^2}{n} = \frac{448 \times 448}{8} = 25{,}088$

Statistical table 1 Distribution of t*

Degrees of freedom	*Deviates necessary to enclose all except the given percentage of frequencies* 60%	40%	20%	10%	5%	2%	1%
1	0·727	1·376	3·078	6·314	12·706	31·821	63·657
2	0·617	1·061	1·886	2·920	4·303	6·965	9·925
3	0·584	0·978	1·638	2·353	3·182	4·541	5·841
4	0·569	0·941	1·533	2·132	2·776	3·747	4·604
5	0·559	0·920	1·476	2·015	2·571	3·365	4·032
6	0·553	0·906	1·440	1·943	2·447	3·143	3·707
7	0·549	0·896	1·415	1·895	2·365	2·998	3·499
8	0·546	0·889	1·397	1·860	2·306	2·896	3·355
9	0·543	0·883	1·383	1·833	2·262	2·821	3·250
10	0·542	0·879	1·372	1·812	2·228	2·764	3·169
11	0·540	0·876	1·363	1·796	2·201	2·718	3·106
12	0·539	0·873	1·356	1·782	2·179	2·681	3·055
13	0·538	0·870	1·350	1·771	2·160	2·650	3·012
14	0·537	0·868	1·345	1·761	2·145	2·624	2·977
15	0·536	0·866	1·341	1·753	2·131	2·602	2·947
16	0·535	0·865	1·337	1·746	2·120	2·583	2·921
17	0·534	0·863	1·333	1·740	2·110	2·567	2·898
18	0·534	0·862	1·330	1·734	2·101	2·552	2·878
19	0·533	0·861	1·328	1·729	2·093	2·539	2·861
20	0·533	0·860	1·325	1·725	2·086	2·528	2·845
21	0·532	0·859	1·323	1·721	2·080	2·518	2·831
22	0·532	0·858	1·321	1·717	2·074	2·508	2·819
23	0·532	0·858	1·319	1·714	2·069	2·500	2·807
24	0·531	0·857	1·318	1·711	2·064	2·492	2·797
25	0·531	0·856	1·316	1·708	2·060	2·485	2·787
26	0·531	0·856	1·315	1·706	2·056	2·479	2·779
27	0·531	0·855	1·314	1·703	2·052	2·473	2·771
28	0·530	0·855	1·313	1·701	2·048	2·467	2·763
29	0·530	0·854	1·311	1·699	2·045	2·462	2·756
30	0·530	0·854	1·310	1·697	2·042	2·457	2·750
60	0·527	0·848	1·296	1·671	2·000	2·390	2·660
120	0·526	0·845	1·289	1·658	1·980	2·358	2·617
∞	0·524	0·842	1·282	1·645	1·960	2·326	2·576

* Adapted from table 3 of Fisher, R. A. and Yates, F., *Statistical Tables for Biological, Agricultural and Medical Research*, Oliver & Boyd, 6th edition 1963, by permission of the authors and publishers.

$$\text{Corrected sum of squares} = \sum x^2 - \frac{(\sum x)^2}{n}$$

$$= 25{,}236 - 25{,}088$$

$$= 148^*$$

We see, then, that a computational formula for the best estimate of the population variance $\hat{\sigma}^2$ may be written as

$$\hat{\sigma}^2 = \frac{\sum x_1^2 - \frac{(\sum x_1)^2}{n_1} + \sum x_2^2 - \frac{(\sum x_2)^2}{n_2}}{n_1 + n_2 - 2} \tag{6}$$

x_1 denoting any score in sample 1, of size n_1, and x_2 any score in sample 2, of size n_2. This may be used in the formula for the estimated standard error of the difference between two means (formula 3) to give

$$\hat{\sigma}_{(M_1 - M_2)} = \sqrt{\left(\frac{\sum x_1^2 - \frac{(\sum x_1)^2}{n_1} + \sum x_2^2 - \frac{(\sum x_2)^2}{n_2}}{n_1 + n_2 - 2}\right)\left(\frac{1}{n_1} + \frac{1}{n_2}\right)} \tag{7}$$

Finally, the formula for the *t* ratio (formula 4) may be rewritten in the computational form

$$t = \frac{M_1 - M_2}{\sqrt{\left(\frac{\sum x_1^2 - \frac{(\sum x_1)^2}{n_1} + \sum x_2^2 - \frac{(\sum x_2)^2}{n_2}}{n_1 + n_2 - 2}\right)\left(\frac{1}{n_1} + \frac{1}{n_2}\right)}} \tag{8}$$

* When, as in the present illustration, all the scores are numerically large, the calculation could be made easier by *coding* the scores, i.e. subtracting a convenient number for all the scores before starting the above procedure. The corrected sum of squares is unaffected by coding. Thus, the reader could verify that if 50 were subtracted from all the scores to give 13, 11, 8, 7, 5, 2, 2 and 0, we would have—using $x_c (= x - 50)$ to denote any coded score—$\sum x_c = 48$, $\sum x_c^2 = 436$, but $\sum x_c^2 - \frac{(\sum x_c)^2}{n} = 148$ as before.

2.3 The assumptions underlying the t test

It is as well to remind ourselves of the assumptions underlying the use of the t distribution in evaluating the statistical significance of the obtained difference between means. These assumptions may be stated as follows:

1. The scores in each of the two populations from which the groups are randomly selected are normally distributed (the assumption of *normality of distribution*).
2. The variances of the scores in the two populations are equal (the assumption of *homogeneity of variance*).
3. The two groups are selected independently.

There is usually no difficulty in being sure whether or not the last assumption holds. Most experiments are planned in such a way that the selection of one group in no way influences that of the other. Again, when related groups are incorporated into the design, a modification of the procedure outlined in section 2.1 is readily available (see, for example, Lewis 1967). (The individuals in the groups could be ordered into 'blocks' as described in the randomized-blocks design, chapter 5.) It is the first two assumptions which now merit more detailed consideration.

It is of little use testing the assumption of normality by the standard tests of skewness and kurtosis, since these tests are insensitive for small samples; i.e. the hypothesis of normality would not be rejected unless the skewness or kurtosis was very pronounced. Similarly, testing the assumption of homogeneity of variance by the F test (discussed in section 2.4) is also of limited value, this test too being insensitive. Of course, even if more sensitive tests were readily available, failure to detect a real difference would not mean that the assumption were necessarily true. A more promising line of investigation is that of demonstrating the effect of violating the assumptions from empirical studies of sampling from populations with known characteristics. A study by Boneau (1960) is of this kind.

Large numbers of ts were calculated—by an electronic computer—from the difference between the means of samples drawn at random from populations which were (a) normal, (b) platykurtic (actually rectangular) and (c) strongly skewed (actually J-shaped with a skew to the right). The means of all the populations were the same, but some had variances four times as large as the others. For different combinations of populations, and for different sample sizes, the percentages of *t*s exceeding the 5-per-cent and 1-per-cent levels were found.

When both populations were normal but had different variances (one four times the other) Boneau found that with samples of 5, 6·4 per cent of the *t*s exceeded the theoretical 5-per-cent limits, and that with samples of 15 the corresponding figure was 4·9 per cent. With different sample sizes, however, (one of 5, the other of 15) only 1 per cent of the *t*s exceeded the 5-per-cent limits when the smaller samples were drawn from the population with the smaller variance, and 16 per cent of the *t*s exceeded these limits when the smaller samples were drawn from the population with the larger variance. A similar pattern was found when the percentage of *t*s exceeded the 1-per-cent limits (see table 2.2). Evidently with populations of unequal variance the discrepancies become important only when the sample sizes are unequal.

When the two populations were strongly skewed (but identical), slightly too few of the calculated *t*s exceeded the theoretical limits, 3·1 per cent exceeding the 5-per-cent for samples of 5, and 4·0 per cent for samples of 15. This is a reassuring result, in that it shows that too many 'significant' *t*s will not be claimed. With two platykurtic populations the discrepancies were negligible. Greater discrepancies occurred, however, when the platykurtic populations differed in variance, 7·1 per cent of the calculated *t*s exceeding the 5-per-cent limits for samples of 5.

Finally, when sampling from two differently shaped populations, such as the normal and skewed populations, Boneau found the distribution of *t*s to be skewed, one of the tails containing a disproportionate share of the frequencies. For samples of 5, for instance, the percentages in the tails defined by the theoretical 5-per-cent limits were 5·6 and 1·5, giving a total of 7·1. When the sample size was increased, however, the disproportion was considerably reduced, as shown in table 2.2B. Nevertheless, it would obviously be foolhardy to apply one-tailed tests of significance to the means of small samples drawn from populations known to be differently skewed.

The general conclusion to be drawn from Boneau's study is that the *t* test of significance is remarkably robust, in that it is affected to but a small extent even by very considerable violations of the assumptions on which it is based. This is especially so if both the samples are the same, or very nearly the same, in size, and if the two population distributions have the same or similar shape. If the sample sizes are not equal, no difficulty arises

Table 2.2 Percentages of *t*s exceeding the theoretical 5-per-cent and 1-per-cent limits in Boneau's study*

A. Sampling from distributions with the same shape

Distribution	*Variances equal (E) or different (D) (ratio* 4:1)	*Sample sizes*†	*Obtained percentage at* 5 *per cent*	1 *per cent*
Normal	*E*	Both 5	6·4	1·8
Normal	*E*	Both 15	4·9	1·1
Normal	*D*	15 and 5	1·0	0·1
Normal	*D*	5 and 15	16·0	6·0
Skewed	*E*	Both 5	3·1	0·3
Skewed	*E*	Both 15	4·0	0·4
Platykurtic	*E*	Both 5	5·1	1·0
Platykurtic	*E*	Both 15	5·0	1·5
Platykurtic	*D*	Both 5	7·1	1·9

B. Sampling from distributions with different shapes (equal variance)

		Obtained percentage at 5 *per cent*		1 *per cent*	
Distribution	*Sample sizes*	*Total*	*Larger tail*	*Total*	*Larger tail*
Skewed and normal	Both 5	7·1	5·6	1·9	1·9
Skewed and normal	Both 15	5·1	4·2	1·4	1·2
Skewed and normal	Both 25	4·6	2·7	1·3	1·1
Skewed and platykurtic	Both 5	6·4	5·0	3·3	2·5
Skewed and platykurtic	Both 15	5·6	3·9	1·6	1·2

* Adapted from the table on p. 61 of *Psychological Bulletin*, **57**, 1, 1960 by permission of the author and the *Psychological Bulletin*.

† If unequal, the size of the samples from the distribution with the larger variance is placed first.

unless the population variances are markedly unequal. It is the combination of unequal sample sizes with (suspected) unequal population variances that must be guarded against. Procedures for dealing with this situation are outlined by Fisher and Yates (1963) and Cochran and Cox (1957).

2.4 The *F* test of significance

The two groups of scores in table 1.1 could also be treated by the more general technique of the *analysis of variance*. It is more general in so far as it can be applied to any number of groups, not just to two. It consists of partitioning the total variation into two or more distinct sources. Thus, the variation of the scores in table 1.1 would be partitioned into two sources, that *between groups* and that *within groups*.

Table 2.3 Alternative analysis of the data in table 1.1

Source of variation	*Sum of squares*	*Degrees of freedom*	*Mean square*
Between groups	49·00	1	49·00
Within groups	264·00	14	18·86
Total	313·00	15	

The within-groups variation would be the sum of the squares of the deviation of the scores from their own group mean, i.e. 148·00 for the scores of the arts group plus 116·00 for the scores of the science group (see table 2.1). This sum, 264·00, does not take any account of the differences between the groups, i.e. the difference between the two group means.

The between-groups variation, on the other hand, takes account of these differences only. It ignores all differences within groups, and consists solely of the variation that would result if each score were replaced by its own group mean. Thus, since the mean of all the sixteen scores in table 1.1 is 54·25, each of the eight arts scores if replaced by their own group mean of 56·00 would give a deviation of 1·75, and each of the eight science scores would in the same way give a deviation of $-1{\cdot}75$. The between-groups variation is therefore $[8 \times 1{\cdot}75^2] + [8 \times (-1{\cdot}75)^2] = 49{\cdot}00$. The analysis can then be set out as in table 2.3.

We see that the sums of the squared deviations—written more shortly as the sums of squares—for between groups and within groups have been added to give a *total* sum of squares. This, which comprises the total variation of the sixteen scores irrespective of grouping, could also have been obtained as the sum of the squares of the deviations of all the scores from the overall mean (54·25). It is, in fact, the corrected sum of squares of the sixteen scores (see section 2.2). The degrees of freedom (see footnote, p. 28), which are 1 for between groups (since there are only two groups) and 14 for within groups (i.e. 7 for each group of eight scores), are likewise added to give 15 for the total. This is clearly correct, since there are sixteen scores in all. The analysis thus resolves both the sum of squares and degrees of freedom into separate components.

The mean squares are obtained by dividing each sum of squares by the appropriate degrees of freedom. That for within groups (18·86) has already been obtained (table 2.1) as an estimate of the population variance assumed to be common to each of the two groups. On the assumption that the means of the two populations also do not differ, the mean square for between groups (49·00) provides a second, and independent, estimate of this same variance, one based solely on the two obtained group means. If, on the other hand, the two populations though still having the same variance have different means, the mean square for between groups then estimates the common population variance plus a component resulting from the difference. Obviously, then, the crucial question is whether the divergence of the two mean squares is great enough to indicate a difference between the population means.

The question is answered by taking the ratio of the two mean squares, known as the F ratio. (It was formerly known as the variance ratio, and was renamed F in honour of R. A. Fisher.) This is because when two estimates of a population variance have been independently obtained from the same population—or, what is essentially the same, from different populations with the same mean and the same variance—then, provided that the distribution of scores in the population(s) is normal, the sampling distribution of the F ratios is known and is given by

$$y = \frac{\nu_1^{\frac{1}{2}\nu_1}\nu_2^{\frac{1}{2}\nu_2}}{B\left(\frac{\nu_1}{2},\frac{\nu_2}{2}\right)} \cdot \frac{F^{\frac{1}{2}(\nu_1-2)}}{(\nu_1 F+\nu_2)^{\frac{1}{2}(\nu_1+\nu_2)}} \tag{9}$$

See Page 40 **

Statistical table 2A Distribution of *F*: 5-per-cent points*

Values of F that would be exceeded in 5 per cent of pairs of random samples of various size combinations

Degrees of freedom for smaller variance	Degrees of freedom for larger variance: 1	2	3	4	5	6	8	12	24	∞
1	161·4	199·5	215·7	224·6	230·2	234·0	238·9	243·9	249·0	254·3
2	18·51	19·00	19·16	19·25	19·30	19·33	19·37	19·41	19·45	19·50
3	10·13	9·55	9·28	9·12	9·01	8·94	8·84	8·74	8·64	8·53
4	7·71	6·94	6·59	6·39	6·26	6·16	6·04	5·91	5·77	5·63
5	6·61	5·79	5·41	5·19	5·05	4·95	4·82	4·68	4·53	4·36
6	5·99	5·14	4·76	4·53	4·39	4·28	4·15	4·00	3·84	3·67
7	5·59	4·74	4·35	4·12	3·97	3·87	3·73	3·57	3·41	3·23
8	5·32	4·46	4·07	3·84	3·69	3·58	3·44	3·28	3·12	2·93
9	5·12	4·26	3·86	3·63	3·48	3·37	3·23	3·07	2·90	2·71
10	4·96	4·10	3·71	3·48	3·33	3·22	3·07	2·91	2·74	2·54
11	4·84	3·98	3·59	3·36	3·20	3·09	2·95	2·79	2·61	2·40
12	4·75	3·88	3·49	3·26	3·11	3·00	2·85	2·69	2·50	2·30
13	4·67	3·80	3·41	3·18	3·02	2·92	2·77	2·60	2·42	2·21
14	4·60	3·74	3·34	3·11	2·96	2·85	2·70	2·53	2·35	2·13
15	4·54	3·68	3·29	3·06	2·90	2·79	2·64	2·48	2·29	2·07
16	4·49	3·63	3·24	3·01	2·85	2·74	2·59	2·42	2·24	2·01
17	4·45	3·59	3·20	2·96	2·81	2·70	2·55	2·38	2·19	1·96
18	4·41	3·55	3·16	2·93	2·77	2·66	2·51	2·34	2·15	1·92
19	4·38	3·52	3·13	2·90	2·74	2·63	2·48	2·31	2·11	1·88
20	4·35	3·49	3·10	2·87	2·71	2·60	2·45	2·28	2·08	1·84
21	4·32	3·47	3·07	2·84	2·68	2·57	2·42	2·25	2·05	1·81
22	4·30	3·44	3·05	2·82	2·66	2·55	2·40	2·23	2·03	1·78
23	4·28	3·42	3·03	2·80	2·64	2·53	2·38	2·20	2·00	1·76
24	4·26	3·40	3·01	2·78	2·62	2·51	2·36	2·18	1·98	1·73
25	4·24	3·38	2·99	2·76	2·60	2·49	2·34	2·16	1·96	1·71
26	4·22	3·37	2·98	2·74	2·59	2·47	2·32	2·15	1·95	1·69
27	4·21	3·35	2·96	2·73	2·57	2·46	2·30	2·13	1·93	1·67
28	4·20	3·34	2·95	2·71	2·56	2·44	2·29	2·12	1·91	1·65
29	4·18	3·33	2·93	2·70	2·54	2·43	2·28	2·10	1·90	1·64
30	4·17	3·32	2·92	2·69	2·53	2·42	2·27	2·09	1·89	1·62
40	4·08	3·23	2·84	2·61	2·45	2·34	2·18	2·00	1·79	1·51
60	4·00	3·15	2·76	2·52	2·37	2·25	2·10	1·92	1·70	1·39
120	3·92	3·07	2·68	2·45	2·29	2·17	2·02	1·83	1·61	1·25
∞	3·84	2·99	2·60	2·37	2·21	2·09	1·94	1·75	1·52	1·00

* Taken from table 5 of Fisher, R. A. and Yates, F., *Statistical Tables for Biological, Agricultural and Medical Research*, Oliver & Boyd, 6th edition 1963, by permission of the authors and publishers.

See Page 40 **

Statistical table 2B Distribution of *F*: 1-per-cent points*

Values of F that would be exceeded in 1 *per cent of pairs of random samples of various size combinations*

Degrees of freedom for smaller variance	*Degrees of freedom for larger variance* 1	2	3	4	5	6	8	12	24	∞
1	4052	4999	5403	5625	5764	5859	5981	6106	6234	6366
2	98·49	99·00	99·17	99·25	99·30	99·33	99·36	99·42	99·46	99·50
3	34·12	30·81	29·46	28·71	28·24	27·91	27·49	27·05	26·60	26·12
4	21·20	18·00	16·69	15·98	15·52	15·21	14·80	14·37	13·93	13·46
5	16·26	13·27	12·06	11·39	10·97	10·67	10·29	9·89	9·47	9·02
6	13·74	10·92	9·78	9·15	8·75	8·47	8·10	7·72	7·31	6·88
7	12·25	9·55	8·45	7·85	7·46	7·19	6·84	6·47	6·07	5·65
8	11·26	8·65	7·59	7·01	6·63	6·37	6·03	5·67	5·28	4·86
9	10·56	8·02	6·99	6·42	6·06	5·80	5·47	5·11	4·73	4·31
10	10·04	7·56	6·55	5·99	5·64	5·39	5·06	4·71	4·33	3·91
11	9·65	7·20	6·22	5·67	5·32	5·07	4·74	4·40	4·02	3·60
12	9·33	6·93	5·95	5·41	5·06	4·82	4·50	4·16	3·78	3·36
13	9·07	6·70	5·74	5·20	4·86	4·62	4·30	3·96	3·59	3·16
14	8·86	6·51	5·56	5·03	4·69	4·46	4·14	3·80	3·43	3·00
15	8·68	6·36	5·42	4·89	4·56	4·32	4·00	3·67	3·29	2·87
16	8·53	6·23	5·29	4·77	4·44	4·20	3·89	3·55	3·18	2·75
17	8·40	6·11	5·18	4·67	4·34	4·10	3·79	3·45	3·08	2·65
18	8·28	6·01	5·09	4·58	4·25	4·01	3·71	3·37	3·00	2·57
19	8·18	5·93	5·01	4·50	4·17	3·94	3·63	3·30	2·92	2·49
20	8·10	5·85	4·94	4·43	4·10	3·87	3·56	3·23	2·86	2·42
21	8·02	5·78	4·87	4·37	4·04	3·81	3·51	3·17	2·80	2·36
22	7·94	5·72	4·82	4·31	3·99	3·76	3·45	3·12	2·75	2·31
23	7·88	5·66	4·76	4·26	3·94	3·71	3·41	3·07	2·70	2·26
24	7·82	5·61	4·72	4·22	3·90	3·67	3·36	3·03	2·66	2·21
25	7·77	5·57	4·68	4·18	3·86	3·63	3·32	2·99	2·62	2·17
26	7·72	5·53	4·64	4·14	3·82	3·59	3·29	2·96	2·58	2·13
27	7·68	5·49	4·60	4·11	3·78	3·56	3·26	2·93	2·55	2·10
28	7·64	5·45	4·57	4·07	3·75	3·53	3·23	2·90	2·52	2·06
29	7·60	5·42	4·54	4·04	3·73	3·50	3·20	2·87	2·49	2·03
30	7·56	5·39	4·51	4·02	3·70	3·47	3·17	2·84	2·47	2·01
40	7·31	5·18	4·31	3·83	3·51	3·29	2·99	2·66	2·29	1·80
60	7·08	4·98	4·13	3·65	3·34	3·12	2·82	2·50	2·12	1·60
120	6·85	4·79	3·95	3·48	3·17	2·96	2·66	2·34	1·95	1·38
∞	6·64	4·60	3·78	3·32	3·02	2·80	2·51	2·18	1·79	1·00

* Taken from table 5 of Fisher, R. A. and Yates, F., ibid., by permission of the authors and publishers.

in which B denotes the beta function as defined in standard texts on the theory of functions.* This distribution is known as the F distribution. We see that it depends on ν_1 and ν_2 as well as on F. ν_1 and ν_2 are the degrees of freedom on which the two variance estimates are based, ν_1 being the degrees of freedom corresponding to the larger of the two variance estimates. There are, therefore, a number of F distributions, one for each combination of the values of ν_1 and ν_2. Generally the distribution of F—like that of t—is unimodal, but is not symmetrical (except when $\nu_1 = \nu_2$), its main features being as shown in figure 2. However, the right-hand tail of the sampling distribution of the Fs defined by $\frac{\hat{\sigma}_1^2}{\hat{\sigma}_2^2}$, ($\hat{\sigma}_1^2$ and $\hat{\sigma}_2^2$ being variance estimates obtained from sample sets 1 and 2) is the same as the left-hand tail of the sampling distribution of the Fs defined by $\frac{\hat{\sigma}_2^2}{\hat{\sigma}_1^2}$. Only one tail of each F distribution need therefore be considered. Statistical tables 2A and B show the values of F that will be exceeded in 5 per cent and 1 per cent of pairs of random samples of various sizes, the F ratio being formed by always placing the larger of the two estimates in the numerator, i.e. the obtained F being necessarily greater than 1. The degrees of freedom for the larger estimate (ν_1) fix the column of the table, and those for the smaller estimates (ν_2) the row.

For the present illustration (table 2.3), therefore, we have, placing the (larger) between-groups mean square in the numerator, $F = \frac{49{\cdot}00}{18{\cdot}86} = 2{\cdot}60$. This is less than the reading in statistical table 2A for 1 and 14 degrees of freedom. The difference between the two mean squares —and hence also between the two group means—is not significant at the 5-per-cent level. Our conclusion, as before, is that the null hypothesis of no difference between the population means must be accepted as tenable.

We should note that if the mean square for between groups happened to be less than that for within groups, the difference would necessarily be a

* The beta function is related to the gamma function (see the t distribution, formula 5) by $B\left(\frac{\nu_1}{2}, \frac{\nu_2}{2}\right) = \frac{\Gamma\left(\frac{\nu_1}{2}\right)\Gamma\left(\frac{\nu_2}{2}\right)}{\Gamma\left(\frac{\nu_1+\nu_2}{2}\right)}$

chance one, and there would be no point in evaluating a F ratio at all. The only alternative to the null hypothesis of no difference between the population means (which implies that the F ratio estimates unity) is that of some difference between the population means (which implies that F defined as the ratio of the mean square for between groups to that for within groups estimates a quantity greater than unity). We should note, too, that the one-tailed nature of this test of significance now makes statistical tables 2A and B relevant as they stand.

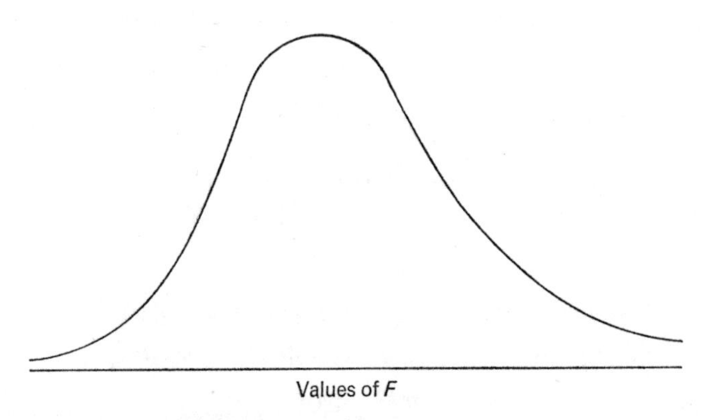

Figure 2 The shape of the F distribution when the degrees of freedom for the larger variance estimate are more than 4.

There is an underlying identity between the two tests of significance. We previously obtained $t = 1{\cdot}61$. The square of this equals the obtained F, apart from rounding errors. The two tests used are essentially the same. The t test, however, is limited to two groups, whereas a F ratio can be derived from an analysis of variance from any number of groups. Illustrations are provided in the following chapters.

2.5 The computation of F

The computations for table 2.3 may be performed by calculating directly from the data (a) the total sum of squares and (b) the between-groups sum of squares. The within-groups sum of squares would then be obtained by subtraction (total sum minus between-groups sum). Moreover, the between-groups sum could be obtained directly from the group totals, i.e. without calculating the group means. Also the total sum of squares, being the corrected sum of squares of all the scores, would be best obtained by the method described in section 2.2. The steps are as follows:

1. Sum of all scores, $\sum x = 63+61+\cdots+47$
   (see table 1.1) $= 868$

2. Correction term, $\dfrac{(\sum x)^2}{n} = \dfrac{868\times 868}{16}$
   $= 47{,}089{\cdot}00$

3. Total sum of squares $= \sum x^2 - \dfrac{(\sum x)^2}{n}$
   $= 63^2+61^2+\cdots+47^2-47{,}089{\cdot}00$
   $= 47{,}402{\cdot}00-47{,}089{\cdot}00$
   $= 313{\cdot}00$

4. Between-groups sum of squares $= \sum \dfrac{(\text{Group sum})^2}{\text{Group size}} - \dfrac{(\sum x)^2}{n}$
   $= \dfrac{448^2}{8}+\dfrac{420^2}{8}-47{,}089{\cdot}00$
   $= 47{,}138{\cdot}00-47{,}089{\cdot}00$
   $= 49{\cdot}00$

5. Within-groups sum of squares $= 313{\cdot}00-49{\cdot}00$
   $= 264{\cdot}00$

F is then obtained from the mean squares derived from these last two sums in the same way as before.

In most cases this mode of procedure will result in a very large saving of arithmetical labour. It can be used whatever the number of groups, and whatever the size of the groups. In particular, the groups need not be the same size. When computing the between-groups sum of squares, we must simply ensure that the square of each group sum is divided by the size of that particular group before adding together the result of all such divisions. The procedure is identical with that outlined above.

2.6 The assumptions underlying the *F* test

As with the *t* test, the assumptions of normality of distribution and homogeneity of variance underly the *F* test of significance. In other words, evaluating the significance of differences from the readings of statistical table 2 assumes that all the groups are randomly selected from normally distributed populations and that the variances of these populations are equal. A number of empirical studies have been made of the effects of violations of these assumptions (e.g. Goddard and Lindquist 1940, Cochran 1947, Norton 1952). Norton's study, which is reported by Lindquist (1956), is a very thorough one and worthy of special note.

Norton sampled from six different populations of cards, three symmetrical (one normal, one leptokurtic and one platykurtic) and three skewed (one slightly skewed, one markedly skewed and one J-shaped). From each of these groups of cards were randomly selected, each group having the same number of cards. A *F* ratio from the sums of squares for between groups and within groups was then obtained. Repeated selections of the same number of groups gave an empirical distribution of *F* ratios. For each of the populations, and for different numbers of groups and group sizes, the percentage of *F*s exceeding the theoretical 5-per-cent and 1-per-cent limits were found. The results are shown in table 2.4A. Evidently the correspondence with the theoretical distribution is in all cases a close one, with 'flatness' or 'peakness' in the form of the distribution more disturbing than lack of symmetry. The *F* test appears to be extremely insensitive to lack of normality—and especially lack of symmetry—in the population, given that the same form of distribution occurs in all the populations sampled.

Norton also investigated the effect of differing population variances, normal population variances of approximately 25, 100 and 225 being selected. In the results shown in table 2.4B, one group from each of these three populations was selected each time. The discrepancies between the empirical and theoretical distributions of *F* are still fairly small. Substantially the same results were obtained when the forms of the distributions (but not the variances) differed. It was only when samples were selected from population distributions differing both in form and variance that the discrepancies become more pronounced. For the results recorded in table 2.4C the differences in variance were extreme—one population variance being more than forty times another!—as well as the differences

Table 2.4 Percentage of *F*s exceeding the theoretical 5-per-cent and 1-per-cent limits in Norton's study*

A. Sampling from distributions with the same shape and equal variances

Distribution	*Number of groups*	*Group size*	*Obtained percentage at 5 per cent*	*Obtained percentage at 1 per cent*
Leptokurtic	3	3	7·83	2·76
Leptokurtic	4	5	6·56	1·63
Platykurtic	3	3	6·07	1·77
Moderately skewed	4	5	5·15	1·32
Markedly skewed	3	3	4·77	0·80
Markedly skewed	4	5	4·76	1·00
J-shaped	3	3	4·80	1·00

B. Sampling from distributions with the same shape and unequal variances

Distribution	*Number of groups*	*Group size*	*Obtained percentage at 5 per cent*	*Obtained percentage at 1 per cent*
Normal	3	3	7·26	2·13
Normal	3	10	6·56	2·00

C. Sampling from distributions with different shapes and unequal variances

Distribution	*Number of groups*	*Group size*	*Obtained percentage at 5 per cent*	*Obtained percentage at 1 per cent*
Normal, moderately skewed, markedly skewed and J-shaped	4	3	10·02	3·57
	4	10	8·10	2·93

* Adapted from tables 4 and 5, pp. 82 and 84, of Lindquist, E. F., *Design and Analysis of Experiments in Psychology and Education*, Houghton Mifflin, 1956, by permission of the publishers.

in form. Such a combination would be expected very infrequently in practice. If we have reason to believe it does occur, statistical table 2 would not be rendered valueless. Thus, for an obtained F exceeding the reading in the 5-per-cent table significance at only 10 per cent could be claimed.

We may reasonably conclude that the F test, like the t test, is remarkably robust. It is insensitive both to lack of normality in the populations and to differing population variances (unless these differences are extreme and are combined with marked differences in form). Because of this robustness it is, in fact, unusual for any check to be made on the normality of distribution unless the departure from normality in the groups sampled is seen to be extreme. Again, it is often unnecessary to test for homogeneity of variance. If, however, an inspection of the scores suggests a lack of homogeneity—a pronounced difference in the group ranges, for instance—a test devised by Bartlett (1937) may be applied. A description of this is postponed until later (section 3.6).

References

BARTLETT, M. S. (1937) 'Some examples of statistical methods of research in agriculture and applied biology,' *Journal of the Royal Statistical Society Supplement*, **4**, 137–70.

BONEAU, C. A. (1960) 'The effects of violations of assumptions underlying the *t* test,' *Psychological Bulletin*, **57**, 49–64.

COCHRAN, W. G. (1947) 'Some consequences when the assumptions for the analysis of variance are not satisfied,' *Biometrics*, **3**, 22–38.

COCHRAN, W. G. and COX, G. M. (1957) *Experimental Designs*, New York: Wiley (2nd edition), pp. 100–2.

FISHER, R. A. and YATES, F. (1963) *Statistical Tables for Biological, Agricultural and Medical Research*, Edinburgh: Oliver & Boyd (6th edition), pp. 3–4.

GODDARD, R. H. and LINDQUIST, E. F. (1940) 'An empirical study of the effect of heterogeneous within-groups variance upon certain *F* tests of significance in analysis of variance,' *Psychometrika*, **5**, 263–74.

LEWIS, D. G. (1967) *Statistical Methods in Education*, London: University of London Press, pp. 119–22.

LINDQUIST, E. F. (1956) *Design and Analysis of Experiments in Psychology and Education*, Boston, Mass.: Houghton Mifflin, pp. 78–86.

NORTON, D. W. (1952) *An Empirical Investigation of Some Effects of Non-normality and Heterogeneity on the F Distribution*, Unpublished Ph.D. thesis, State University of Iowa.

Chapter 3 Designs with Randomized Groups

3.1 A simple methods experiment

We begin by considering a basic design, that of randomized groups as exemplified by a simple methods experiment. Although this design in itself has very limited application in educational research, it is of fundamental importance in that it provides the basis for designs which are of direct usefulness. It is vital, therefore, that a thorough understanding of the randomized-groups design be achieved in the first place.

Suppose that we are interested in the relative effectiveness of four methods of teaching a certain topic in a particular school. We select four random groups of pupils, and allocate each group to one of the methods. The pupils, we will suppose, are all from one age group, the age at which we wish to investigate the effectiveness of the methods. Otherwise the groups are selected solely by chance, e.g. by the use of tables of random numbers. Again, if the groups are taught by different teachers, the allocation of the teachers to the groups must be solely by chance. Alternatively, all the groups could be taught by the same teacher. After the lesson, or series of lessons, the same test is administered to all four groups. We will suppose in this illustration that there are six pupils in each of the groups, and that the test scores obtained are as shown in table 3.1.

A comparison of the mean scores for the four groups suggests differences between the effectiveness of the methods. The *F* ratio, provided by an analysis of variance, enables us to test the significance of the differences. We proceed with the calculation as follows:

1. Overall sum of scores, $\sum x = 117+150+165+168$

$$= 600$$

$$\left(\text{The overall mean is therefore } \frac{600}{24} = 25{\cdot}0\right)$$

2. Correction term,
$$\frac{(\sum x)^2}{N} = \frac{600 \times 600}{24} = 15{,}000$$

3. Total sum of squares
$$= (26^2 + 23^2 + 19^2 + \cdots + 22^2) - 15{,}000$$
Sum of 24 terms
$$= 15{,}718 - 15{,}000 = 718$$

4. Between-groups sum of squares
$$= \frac{117^2}{6} + \frac{150^2}{6} + \frac{165^2}{6} + \frac{168^2}{6} - 15{,}000$$
$$= 15{,}273 - 15{,}000 = 273$$

5. Within-groups sum of squares
$$= 718 - 273 = 445$$

Table 3.1 Scores of four method groups, with six pupils in each group

	Method groups			
	1	2	3	4
	26	32	37	35
	23	28	30	29
	19	26	27	29
	17	24	26	28
	17	21	23	25
	15	19	22	22
Group sum	117	150	165	168
Group mean	19·5	25·0	27·5	28·0

The total sum of squares (718) gives a measure of the variation of the scores not taking any account of their separation into groups. It is, in fact, the sum of the squares of all the scores expressed as deviations from the overall mean (25·0). The degrees of freedom are 23, 1 less than the total number of scores.

The between-groups sum (273) expresses only the variation between groups. It gives a measure of the variation that would result if each score were replaced by the mean of the group to which it belongs. It is, in fact, the sum of the squares of the four group means, expressed as deviations from the overall mean, increased sixfold (since there are six scores in each group). Thus, the sum of the squared deviations of the group mean is

$$
\begin{aligned}
& (19{\cdot}5-25{\cdot}0)^2+(25{\cdot}0-25{\cdot}0)^2+(27{\cdot}5-25{\cdot}0)^2+(28{\cdot}0-25{\cdot}0)^2 \\
= \;& 5{\cdot}5^2 \quad + \quad 0^2 \quad + \quad 2{\cdot}5^2 \quad + \quad 3^2 \\
= \;& 45{\cdot}50
\end{aligned}
$$

and this, multiplied by 6 gives the between-groups sum of squares, 273. The degrees of freedom are 3, 1 less than the number of groups.

Table 3.2 Analysis of variance of the data in table 3.1

Source of variation	*Sum of squares*	*Degrees of freedom*	*Mean square*
Between groups (methods)	273	3	91·00
Within groups	445	20	22·25
Total	718	23	

The within-groups sum (445), obtained above by subtraction, could also have been obtained from first principles (see p. 36) as the sum of the squares of all the scores expressed as deviations from their own group mean. The degrees of freedom, also obtained by subtraction ($23-3 = 20$), could also be derived from summing the 5 degrees of freedom for each of the separate groups.

The three sums of squares together with their degrees of freedom are set out in table 3.2. The resulting mean square, or variance estimate, for between groups and within groups is also shown. The ratio of the mean square for between groups to that for within groups is then obtained as $F = \dfrac{91{\cdot}00}{22{\cdot}25} = 4{\cdot}09$. This exceeds the reading in statistical table 2A for 3 and 20 degrees of freedom (3·10). We conclude that the differences among the group means are significant at the 5-per-cent level. It is improbable that chance alone accounts for the obtained differences between the effectiveness of the methods.

It is well to appreciate the limitations in our conclusion. This conclusion —that the differences among the methods may reasonably be considered non-chance—relates only to the pupils of the given year-group within the particular school, and to the methods as taught by the teachers in that school. Indeed, if all the methods have been taught by the same teacher, the significance of the method differences relates only to the methods as taught by that teacher. And if, on the other hand, the groups have been taught by different teachers randomly selected from a panel of teachers in the school, the significance of the differences relates to the methods as taught by members of that panel. To generalize to pupils from other schools (who may have grown used to different teaching methods—methods that would affect their response to the particular methods investigated) is not permissible. This is why a randomized-groups design, such as that employed in a simple methods experiment, has few direct applications in educational research.

A second limitation concerns the nature of the test of significance. It is an *overall* test, one assessing the differences among the groups as a whole. It does not follow that the difference between any particular two group means is significant at the same level. Differences between particular groups must be considered separately.

3.2 Comparisons of particular groups

Once the F ratio has indicated real differences among the group means, the significance of the differences between any two group means could be tested by the t ratio. We need not, however, proceed again from the beginning. The within-groups mean square can usually be taken as an estimate (and one based on all the available data) of the population variance for each of the groups. (This implies that the assumption of homogeneity of variance extends over *all* the groups, not just the particular two groups we are considering.) The standard error of the difference between the group means is then estimated by

$$\hat{\sigma}_{(M_1-M_2)} = \sqrt{\frac{2\hat{\sigma}^2}{n}} \qquad (10)$$

where $\hat{\sigma}^2$ is the within-groups mean square, and n is the size of the group. The formula corresponds to formula (3), p. 27, where both n_1 and n_2 are replaced by n. In this illustration, then, the standard error is evaluated as $\sqrt{\frac{2 \times 22{\cdot}25}{6}} = 2{\cdot}72$. With d referring to an obtained difference in means, we would then have $t = \frac{d}{2{\cdot}72}$, and this would be compared with the t ratio for 20 degrees of freedom (the same number as that on which the estimate $\hat{\sigma}^2$ is based) in statistical table 1.

Alternatively, starting from statistical table 1 we see that a t ratio of 3·10 is necessary for significance at the 5-per-cent level. Putting $t = 3{\cdot}10$, we then have $3{\cdot}10 = \frac{d}{2{\cdot}72}$, whence $d = 3{\cdot}10 \times 2{\cdot}72 = 8{\cdot}43$, so giving the *minimum* difference between group means for significance at the 5-per-cent level. Of the six differences between the four group means shown in table 3.1, only one, that between the means of groups 1 and 4, exceeds this. Only this difference, therefore, is significant at the 5-per-cent level.

Generally, claiming significance at any given level of *one* difference in this way is justifiable only if the significance of the overall differences has first been established at that level. We should not, for instance, begin by selecting the largest difference and testing its significance by the t ratio. The largest difference (and also, for that matter, other differences) might well be significant at, say, the 5-per-cent level without the overall differences being significant at this level.* We could justifiably test a particular difference in group means (irrespective of the significance of the overall differences) only if we have a special interest in contrasting the two methods concerned, i.e. the methods stand out as meriting particular attention when the experiment is being planned. We must, of course, beware of discovering a special interest in the two methods only *after* the group means have been obtained!

When the number of groups is large, testing the significance of particular differences by the t test in the way described is open to criticism, even when the significance of the overall differences (at the same level) has first

* Statistical table 1 gives the probability of obtaining various values of t from single random sample pairs, not the probability of obtaining values of t as the largest of a number of random sample pairs.

been established. This is because, just as when the evidence indicates no real differences (the overall null hypothesis being accepted), *some* of the separate differences must none the less be expected to exceed the minimum difference for significance—5 per cent of the differences exceeding the minimum difference for 5-per-cent significance—so when real differences are indicated, slightly more than the allowed percentage of the separate differences must be expected to exceed the minimum difference as calculated above. In other words, a slightly more stringent test for the significance of the separate differences would be desirable. Readers who may have to deal with a large number of groups in this way should consult the tests provided by Tukey (1953), a modification of which is described by Snedecor (1956, pp. 251–3), and Scheffé (1953). Discussions by Federer (1955) and Ryan (1959) are also of interest.

The qualification just discussed does not, of course, apply to special comparisons suggested by the nature of the methods themselves; nor does it apply if a comparison between a particular method and a combination of other methods is suggested. Suppose, for example, that all four methods of the present illustration relate to the effect of practice and coaching on improving test performance, and that method 1 is unique in that it involves no special preparation of any kind. (The method 1 group, in other words, serves as a control.) We will suppose that the methods are as follows:

Method 1: no practice or coaching.
Method 2: practice only.
Method 3: practice plus slight coaching.
Method 4: practice plus intense coaching.

It would then be justifiable, irrespective of the value of the F ratio, to compare method 1 with methods 2, 3 and 4 combined. This involves a partitioning of the between-groups variation shown in table 3.2 into two components, one based on the difference between method 1 and the other methods combined, and the other on the differences of the other methods among themselves. For the former component the sum of squares is

$$\begin{aligned} &\frac{117^2}{6}+\frac{(150+165+168)^2}{18}-15{,}000 \\ &= 15{,}242-15{,}000 \\ &= 242 \end{aligned}$$

This sum has 1 degree of freedom, being based on the difference between *two* means, that for group 1 and that for groups 2, 3 and 4 combined. For the differences among methods 2, 3 and 4 the sum of squares is

$$\frac{150^2}{6}+\frac{165^2}{6}+\frac{168^2}{6}-\frac{(150+165+168)^2}{18}$$
$$= 12{,}991{\cdot}5-12{,}960{\cdot}5$$
$$= 31{\cdot}0$$

More shortly, this could have been obtained by subtraction, 273−242. The degrees of freedom are 2, as the sum is based on the difference between three groups.

Table 3.3 Further analysis of the data in table 3.1

Source of variation	*Sum of squares*	*Degrees of freedom*	*Mean square*
Between groups 1 and groups 2, 3 and 4	242	1	242·00
Among groups 2, 3 and 4	31	2	15·50
Within groups	445	20	22·25
Total	718	23	

The full analysis is set out in table 3.3. We see that the greater part of the former between-groups variation (table 3.2) now appears between group 1 and the rest, the ratio of the mean square to that for within groups being $F = \frac{242{\cdot}00}{22{\cdot}25} = 10{\cdot}88$. This exceeds the reading in statistical table 2B for 1 and 20 degrees of freedom (8·10). The difference is significant at the 1-per-cent level. We may reasonably conclude that the methods involving practice have a real superiority over method 1.

The variation among methods 2, 3 and 4, on the other hand, is small and statistically insignificant $\left(F = \frac{15{\cdot}50}{22{\cdot}25} < 1\right)$. The results fail to establish a real difference (overall) among the methods involving practice. Despite this, however, we could well argue for a test of significance contrasting method 2—the one method of the three *not* involving coaching —with methods 3 and 4 combined. Such a test would involve a further partitioning of the between-groups variation, one in which the sum of squares for differences among groups 2, 3 and 4, 31·00, is split into two components. One component would be based on the difference between method 2 and methods 3 and 4 combined, and the other on the difference between methods 3 and 4. For the former component the sum of squares is

$$\frac{150^2}{6}+\frac{(165+168)^2}{12}-\frac{(150+165+168)^2}{18}$$
$$= 12{,}990{\cdot}75-12{,}960{\cdot}50$$
$$= 30{\cdot}25$$

This sum has 1 degree of freedom, being based on the difference between two means, that for group 2 and that for groups 3 and 4 combined. For the latter component the sum of squares is

$$\frac{165^2}{6}+\frac{168^2}{6}-\frac{(165+168)^2}{12}$$
$$= 9{,}241{\cdot}50-9{,}240{\cdot}75$$
$$= 0{\cdot}75$$

Again, this could have been obtained more simply by subtraction, i.e. 31·00 − 30·25. This sum also has 1 degree of freedom. The complete analysis is set out in table 3.4.

Table 3.4 Still further analysis of the data in table 3.1

Source of variation	*Sum of squares*	*Degrees of freedom*	*Mean square*
Between group 1 and groups 2, 3 and 4	242·00	1	242·00
Between group 2 and groups 3 and 4	30·25	1	30·25
Between groups 3 and 4	0·75	1	0·75
Within groups	445·00	20	22·25
Total	718·00	23	

Almost all the variation among groups 2, 3 and 4 now appears between group 2 and groups 3 and 4. Even so, the ratio of the mean square to that for within groups is only $F = \frac{30 \cdot 25}{22 \cdot 25} = 1 \cdot 36$, as compared with the ratio of 4·35 necessary for significance at the 5-per-cent level (see statistical table 2A). Clearly the effect of coaching additional to that of practice has not been established. And of even less statistical significance is the effect of intensive coaching, since the corresponding ratio for the difference between groups 3 and 4 is $F = \frac{0 \cdot 75}{22 \cdot 25} < 1$.

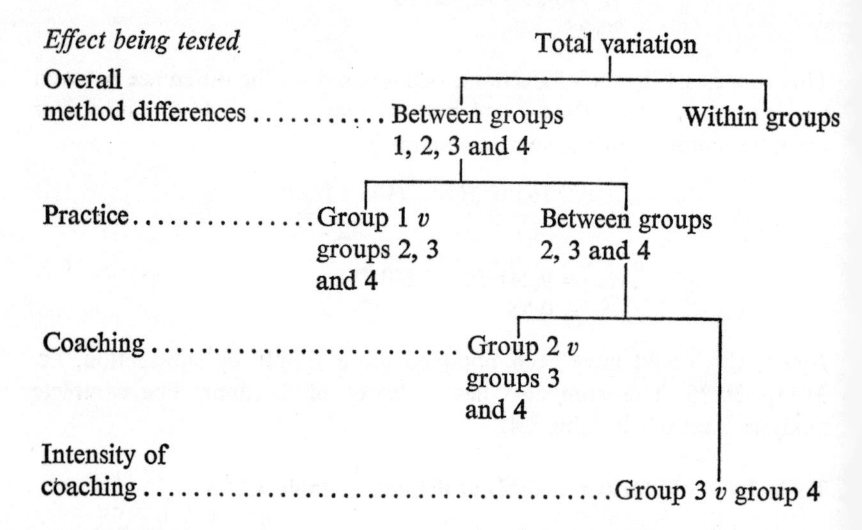

Figure 3 Breakdown of variation in a methods experiment. (Group 1 receives neither practice nor coaching, group 2 receives practice, group 3 receives practice plus slight coaching, and group 4 receives practice plus intensive coaching.)

The complete breakdown of the variation is shown in figure 3. We should emphasize that this breakdown was suggested from the nature of the 'methods' themselves. It was an integral part of the design. Such designed comparisons should be made whenever possible, as they are more likely to lead to the detection of real differences than the indiscriminate testing of differences among the separate group means. A further, more general description of special comparisons is provided in section 3.5.

3.3 The general model

We must now make an explicit statement of what is involved in the analysis of variance used in the methods experiment described. A basic assumption is that any pupil's score can be regarded as made of three parts, namely:

1. A part common to all the scores.
2. A part characteristic of the particular method (and therefore common to the scores of all pupils in the particular method group).
3. A part characteristic of the particular pupil.

It is also assumed that the parts are independent and additive. We can therefore express the assumption in algebraic shorthand by saying that the score x_{ij} of the jth pupil in the ith method consists of independent components as follows:

$$x_{ij} = M + A_i + e_{ij} \tag{11}$$

where M is a component common to all the scores;
A_i is component common to all scores in method i;
and e_{ij} is a component specific to pupil j of method i.
(In the particular experiment described i would run from 1 to 4, there being four groups in all, and j would run from 1 to 6, there being six scores in each of the groups.)

Without loss of generality we may put A_i equal to the population mean of the scores for method i—i.e. the mean of the hypothetical population of scores that would result if all the original population of pupils (the population from which *all* the groups were originally selected) had undergone the 'treatment' of method i—and express this as a deviation from the mean of the population means for all the methods.* It then follows that, summing for all the methods, $\sum A_i = 0$. Equally without loss of generality we may put M equal to the mean of the population means for all the methods.

To revert to table 3.1, therefore, the overall mean 25·0 would be an estimate of M, while the separate group means, expressed as deviations

* It is essential to distinguish between the hypothetical populations of scores, one for each of the method groups, and the original or parent population of pupils from which all the groups were originally selected. The F test may then be regarded as a test of the tenability of the null hypothesis that all the treatment populations have the same mean and the same variance, this common variance being estimated by the within-groups mean square.

from 25·0, would be estimates of the A_is, i.e. $19{\cdot}5-25{\cdot}0 = -5{\cdot}5$ would be an estimate of A_1, $25{\cdot}0-25{\cdot}0 = 0$ would be an estimate of A_2, $27{\cdot}5-25{\cdot}0 = 2{\cdot}5$ would be an estimate of A_3, and $28{\cdot}0-25{\cdot}0 = 3{\cdot}0$ would be an estimate of A_4.

The part e_{ij} represents the element of randomness essential to every design. Since $M+A_i$ already denotes the population mean of the scores for method i, it follows that e_{ij} must be regarded—and for each value of i in turn—as a random deviation from zero. (In other words, summing with respect to j for the population would give $\sum_j e_{ij} = 0$ for each in turn.) We also assume that, for any given i, e_{ij} is from a normally distributed population of scores with a variance *which is the same for all the populations*, i.e. all values of i in turn. We shall denote this common population variance by σ^2.

Thus, to revert again to table 3.1, $26-19{\cdot}5 = 6{\cdot}5$ estimates e_{11}, $23-19{\cdot}5 = 4{\cdot}5$ estimates e_{12}, $19-19{\cdot}5 = -0{\cdot}5$ estimates e_{13}, and so on. Note that the six estimates of $e_{11}, e_{12}, \cdots e_{16}$ sum to zero only because we have used the group mean 19·5 as an estimate of $M+A_1$. The exact value of $e_{11}, e_{12}, \cdots e_{16}$ would not sum to zero unless $M+A_1$ happened to be 19·5. But the sum of all the possible e_{ij}s would still be zero. Similarly, the actual variance of the group scores—and also of the scores from any other group—only estimates σ^2. (The best estimate is provided by the within-groups mean square, 22·25.) But if, as we assume, the variance of the scores *of each group* estimates σ^2, it follows that these variances must differ only by chance.

We have stated that the within-groups mean square estimates σ^2. It can be shown that the between-groups mean square estimates σ^2 plus a component due to the variation of the population means A_i. And with k groups in all, and n scores in each group, this added component is $\dfrac{n\sum_i A_i^2}{k-1}$.

In other words

$$F \text{ estimates } \qquad \frac{\sigma^2+\dfrac{n\sum_i A_i^2}{k-1}}{\sigma^2}$$

The null hypothesis of no differences among the population means is that $\sum A_i^2 = 0$ (since the A_is are in deviation form, no differences imply that each A_i is zero), so that the added component is also zero. If the hypothesis is true, therefore, F estimates 1. Conversely, if the hypothesis is false, F estimates a quantity greater than 1. In practice, of course, we do not know what F estimates. We only know F. Statistical table 2, however, provides the probability of values of F greater than 1 arising from sampling when the null hypothesis is true. If it so happens that the obtained F is less than 1, the between-groups mean square being less than that for within groups, the difference from 1 is necessarily due to chance and the null hypothesis is accepted.

$\frac{\sum_i A_i^2}{k-1}$ has the familiar form of a variance estimate. It would, in fact, be the estimated variance of the population—if such a population could exist—from which $A_1, A_2, \cdots A_k$ is itself a sample. It would not, in fact, be very meaningful to regard the A_is of a methods experiment as a random sample of a population (and theoretically an infinitely large population) in this way. The particular methods compared would not, of course, be the only possible methods, but we could expect them to be—in the opinion of the experimenter, at any rate—the best of a relatively small number. They would not be regarded as a random sample from a large number of methods. And if the experiment were to be repeated with different groups of pupils, precisely the same methods would be used again (and so the A_is would be unchanged). We describe this by saying that we have a *fixed-effects* model. The methods are not subject to sampling.

In contrast, however, we could conduct experiments, with the same randomized-groups design, in which the basis of the group classification—that which corresponds to the methods of a methods experiment—*is* subject to sampling. We could, for instance, test one group of pupils from each of a number of different, and randomly selected, schools. It would then be appropriate to regard the A_is—now the population means from the *particular* schools—as a random sample of a population of similar means. And if the experiment were to be repeated, not only different pupils but also different schools would be used. The model would now be said to have *random effects*. For such a model it would be sensible to replace $\frac{\sum_i A_i^2}{k-1}$ by σ_A^2, σ^2 being the accepted symbol for a population variance and the subscript A showing that this variance derives from the variation not of individuals but of entire groups.

There is no reason why this replacement should not also be made for a fixed-effects model, provided we appreciate that then the replacement is a formal one only. Some writers insist on retaining the form $\frac{\sum_i A_i^2}{k-1}$ for fixed-effects models, while others prefer different symbols, such as κ_A^2 or θ_A^2. To the present writer this seems unnecessarily pedantic. The advantages of using the form σ_A^2 throughout, whether the basis of group classification is subject to sampling or not, will be apparent when more complicated designs are described.*

Table 3.5 Components analysis for a randomized-groups design

Source of variation	*Degrees of freedom*†	*Mean-square expectation*
Groups (A)	$k-1$	$\sigma^2+n\sigma_A^2$
Individual	$k(n-1)$	σ^2
Total	$kn-1$	

† It is assumed that there are k groups, each of size n.

We therefore write the parameters estimated by the mean square of the two independent sources of variation in a randomized-groups design (individuals and groups) as shown in the last column of table 3.5. A component analysis such as this will be found to be indispensable for testing the significance of different sources of variation in the more complex designs described later in the book.

3.4 Groups of unequal size

So far we have assumed all the groups of a randomized-groups design to be of the same size, n. This, however, is an unnecessary restriction. While

* A further point is that both the fixed-effects and random-effects models may be conceived mathematically as special cases of a *general finite model*, where the group A_is are samples from a finite, and not necessarily large, population (see Wilk and Kempthorne 1955).

it is more *convenient* to use groups of the same size whenever possible, the method of analysis could equally well be employed with groups of different sizes.

As far as the computation of the sums of squares is concerned, all that need be especially noted is that in calculating the between-groups sum the square of each group sum must be divided by its own group size (n_i). Thus, for the data recorded in table 3.6 the between-groups sum of squares would be

$$\underbrace{\frac{180^2}{6}+\frac{183^2}{5}+\cdots+\frac{280^2}{9}}_{\text{Sum of 7 terms}}-\frac{(180+183+\cdots+280)^2}{49}$$

$= 510{\cdot}20$

Table 3.6 Scores of seven groups of unequal size

	Groups 1	2	3	4	5	6	7
	35	40	36	33	29	31	37
	32	38	34	32	25	30	37
	31	36	33	32	24	28	34
	30	35	31	30	24	25	32
	27	34	29	28	24	23	31
	25		28	26	22	23	28
			26	24		21	28
			25				27
			24				26
Group sum	180	183	266	205	148	181	280
Group size (n_i)	6	5	9	7	6	7	9
Group mean	30·00	36·60	29·56	29·29	24·67	25·86	31·11

The total and within-groups sums would be obtained in precisely the same way as before (p. 42). The reader may wish to verify that the analysis of variance would be as shown in table 3.7. The degrees of freedom for within groups, obtained as before by subtraction, would also result from summing n_i-1 (i.e. group size minus 1) for all the groups, and is therefore equal to $N-k$, where N is the total number of scores and k the number of groups. For this example, therefore, the degrees of freedom for within groups would result from

$$\sum(n_i-1) = 5+4+\cdots+8 = 42$$

The F ratio is $\frac{85\cdot03}{13\cdot00} = 6\cdot54$, as compared with the reading of 3·27 from statistical table 2B for 6 and 42 degrees of freedom. The differences among the group means are significant at the 1-per-cent level.

Table 3.7 Analysis of variance of the data in table 3.6

Source of variation	*Sum of squares*	*Degrees of freedom*	*Mean square*
Between groups	510·20	6	85·03
Within groups	545·93	42	13·00
Total	1,056·13	48	

The general model would be written as

$$x_{ij} = M+A_i+e_{ij}$$

where all the symbols have the same meaning as before (equation 11, p. 55) except that j now runs from 1 to n_i, with i running from 1 to k as before.

In the components analysis, the term σ_A^2 must now be multiplied by *an average* of the n_is in the mean-square expectation for groups (see table 3.5). The correct average (n_{av}) is given by

$$n_{av} = \frac{1}{k-1}\left(\sum n_i - \frac{\sum n_i^2}{\sum n_i}\right) \tag{12}$$

where $\sum n_i$ is the sum of the group sizes, and $\sum n_i^2$ the sum of the squares of the group sizes.* For the data in table 3.6 we therefore have

* See Kempthorne (1952). If, of course, all the groups are the same size, i.e. $n_i = n$ for all i, n_{av} reduces to n.

$$\sum n_i = 6+5+ \cdots +9 = 49$$

and

$$\sum n_i^2 = 36+25+ \cdots +81 = 357$$

so that

$$n_{av} = \frac{1}{6}\left(49 - \frac{357}{49}\right) = 6{\cdot}95$$

The components analysis for the general case of groups of unequal size is shown in table 3.8.

Table 3.8 Components analysis for a randomized-groups design with groups of unequal size

Source of variation	*Degrees of freedom**	*Mean-square expectation†*
Groups (A)	$k-1$	$\sigma^2 + n_{av}\sigma_A^2$
Individuals	$N-k$	σ^2
Total	$N-1$	

* There are N scores in all, distributed over k groups.

† $n_{av} = \dfrac{1}{k-1}\left[\Sigma n_i - \dfrac{\Sigma n_i^2}{\Sigma n_i}\right]$, n_i being the number of scores in the ith group.

3.5 Orthogonal comparisons

Earlier in this chapter some designed comparisons between the groups of a methods experiment were described. We saw that the between-groups sum of squares of an analysis of variance which had 3 degrees of freedom (table 3.2) was replaced by three components, each with 1 degree of freedom (table 3.4). Each of these components was based on a comparison between two or more of the method groups. Whenever we have a number of different method or 'treatment' groups, it is possible to analyse the between-groups sum of squares into separate components, each with a single degree of freedom, in this way. Indeed, with three or more groups such an analysis may be made in several ways, though whether more than one way would be of interest in any particular experiment is another matter.

Suppose, then, that we have k different 'treatment' groups, all of the same size n. (The modifications necessary when the number of scores in the groups differs will be described afterwards.) Let the group sums be denoted by $S_1, S_2, \cdots S_k$. Any linear function of the group sums may then be written as

$$c = \lambda_1 S_1 + \lambda_2 S_2 + \cdots + \lambda_k S_k$$

where $\lambda_1, \lambda_2, \cdots \lambda_k$ are the coefficients of the sums. This function may be described as a *comparison* of the group sums (and therefore also of the group means) if the sum of the coefficients is zero, i.e. if $\sum \lambda = 0$.

As an example we may take the comparison of the group sums of the methods experiment, in which group 1 is compared with the other three groups combined (table 3.3). Here the comparison is essentially that of S_1 with the mean of S_2, S_3 and S_4, i.e. S_1 with $\frac{1}{3}(S_2+S_3+S_4)$. This is the same as comparing $3S_1$ with $S_2+S_3+S_4$. We therefore put $\lambda_1 = 3$, and each of λ_2, λ_3 and λ_4 equal to -1. Again, when comparing group 2 with groups 3 and 4, we would put $\lambda_1 = 0$ (since group 1 does not enter into the comparison), $\lambda_2 = 2$, and λ_3 and λ_4 both equal to -1. Note that there would be no point in comparing S_1 with $S_2+S_3+S_4$, or S_2 with S_3+S_4. Our interest would always be confined to situations in which the sum of the coefficients is zero.

Our reason for thinking of a comparison in terms of λ coefficients in this way is that the sum of squares may be written down straight away. The sum of squares for any comparison is

$$\frac{c^2}{n \sum \lambda^2}$$

Thus, for the group 1 *v* groups 2, 3 and 4 comparison in the methods experiment (see table 3.1) the sum of squares would be

$$\frac{(3\times 117-150-165-168)^2}{6\times 12} = 242, \text{ as shown in table 3.3.}$$

Again for the group 2 *v* groups 3 and 4 comparison the sum is

$$\frac{(2\times 150-165-168)^2}{6\times 6} = 30{\cdot}25, \text{ as shown in table 3.4.}$$

Contrast this with the previous method of calculation (pp. 51 and 53).

In each denominator 6 is the number of scores in each group. The second factor, $\sum \lambda^2$, is obtained as $3^2+(-1)^2+(-1)^2+(-1)^2$ in the first comparison, and as $2^2+(-1)^2+(-1)^2$ in the second.

Two comparisons are said to be *orthogonal*, or *independent*, if the sum of the products of the corresponding coefficients is zero, i.e. if the comparisons are

$$c_1 = \lambda_{11} S_1 + \lambda_{12} S_2 + \cdots + \lambda_{1k} S_k$$

and

$$c_2 = \lambda_{21} S_1 + \lambda_{22} S_2 + \cdots + \lambda_{2k} S_k$$

then they are orthogonal if

$$\lambda_{11}\lambda_{21} + \lambda_{12}\lambda_{22} + \cdots + \lambda_{1k}\lambda_{2k} = 0 \tag{13}$$

The two comparisons of the methods experiment referred to above are orthogonal, since $(3)(0)+(-1)(2)+(-1)(-1)+(-1)(-1) = 0$. Indeed, any two of the three designed comparisons described for this experiment are orthogonal, as may be seen from the coefficients set out below.

Comparison	*Groups* 1	2	3	4
c_1	3	−1	−1	−1
c_2	0	2	−1	−1
c_3	0	0	1	−1

The importance of orthogonality in three or more comparisons is that the sum of squares for a second orthogonal comparison is part of the *residual* of the between-groups sum, i.e. it is a component of that part of the between-groups sum left after the removal of the sum for the first comparison; and the sum of squares for a third comparison, orthogonal to both the other two, is a component of that part of the between-groups sum left after the removal of the sums for the first and second comparisons; and so on. In other words, if with k groups in all, we select $k-1$ comparisons mutually orthogonal, then

$$\frac{c_1^2}{n\sum\lambda_1^2} + \frac{c_2^2}{n\sum\lambda_2^2} + \cdots + \frac{c_{k-1}^2}{n\sum\lambda_{k-1}^2} = \begin{cases}\text{Between-groups}\\ \text{sum of squares}\end{cases}$$

This has already been illustrated for $k = 4$ groups by the three mutually orthogonal comparisons described for the methods experiment, since

$$242{\cdot}00+30{\cdot}25+0{\cdot}75 = 273{\cdot}00$$

which is the between-groups (or methods) sum of squares in table 3.2.

It is possible to partition the between-groups sum of squares into more than one set of mutually orthogonal comparisons. Thus, coefficients for another set of orthogonal comparisons for four treatment groups are shown below.

	Groups			
Comparison	1	2	3	4
c_1'	1	1	−1	−1
c_2'	1	−1	1	−1
c_3'	1	−1	−1	1

As before, we see that the sum of the coefficients in each row is zero, and that for any two of the rows the sum of the products of corresponding coefficients is also zero.

The following experiment is one for which these comparisons would be of interest. Two different approaches to the teaching of reading could be investigated—a phonetic approach and a 'look-and-say' approach, for instance—using reading material in either the augmented roman alphabet or the traditional orthography. Four independently selected, random groups could then be tested for reading attainment after the following 'treatments':

Group 1: phonetic approach, with traditional orthography.
Group 2: 'look-and-say' approach, with traditional orthography.
Group 3: phonetic approach, with augmented roman alphabet.
Group 4: 'look-and-say' approach, with augmented roman alphabet.

Comparison c_1' would then compare the suitability of the two types of reading material; the second comparison c_2' would compare the effectiveness of the two approaches; and the third comparison c_3' would compare the differences in the effectiveness of the two approaches with each type of material. This last comparison is necessary, since it would be unwise to assume that any difference between the approaches would be unaffected by the reading material.

Table 3.9 An illustration of Bartlett's test of homogeneity of variance. Sums of squares derived from scores in table 3.6

Group	*Sums of squares (within groups)*	*Degrees of freedom*	$\frac{1}{(n_i-1)}$	*Mean square* (S_i^2)	$\log S_i^2$	$(n_i-1)\log S_i^2$
1	64·00	5	0·2000	12·800	1·1072	5·5360
2	23·20	4	0·2500	5·800	0·7634	3·0536
3	142·22	8	0·1250	17·778	1·2500	10·0000
4	69·43	6	0·1667	11·572	1·0633	6·3798
5	27·33	5	0·2000	5·466	0·7377	3·6885
6	78·86	6	0·1667	13·143	1·1186	6·7116
7	140·89	8	0·1250	17·611	1·2457	9·9656
$k = 7$	545·93	42	1·2334			45·3351
	↑	↑	↑			↑
	Σx^2	$\Sigma(n_i-1)$	$\sum \frac{1}{(n_i-1)}$			$\Sigma(n_i-1)\log S_i$

$$\text{Mean square, } S_w^2 = \frac{\Sigma x^2}{\Sigma(n_i-1)} = \frac{545·93}{42} = 13·00$$

$$\Sigma(n_i-1)\log S_w^2 = 42 \times \log 13·00 = 42 \times 1·1139 = 46·7838$$

$$\chi^2 = 2·3026\,[\Sigma(n_i-1)\log S_w^2 - \Sigma(n_i-1)\log S_i]$$

$$= 2·3026\,[46·7838 - 45·3351] = 3·358$$

$$\text{Correction factor, } C = 1 + \frac{1}{3(k-1)}\left[\sum\frac{1}{(n_i-1)} - \frac{1}{\Sigma(n_i-1)}\right]$$

$$= 1 + \frac{1}{3 \times 6}\left[1·2334 - \frac{1}{42}\right] = 1·0672$$

$$\text{Corrected } \chi^2 = \frac{3·358}{1·0672} = 3·146; \quad \text{degrees of freedom, } k-1 = 7$$

In some experiments it might be unnecessary to make all the comparisons: only some of the $k-1$ comparisons might be of interest. It is always more efficient, however, to incorporate whatever comparisons are of interest in a set of mutually orthogonal comparisons whenever this is possible.

Modifications for unequal groups

If the k groups do not contain equal numbers of scores, then the linear function of the group sums

$$c = \lambda_1 S_1 + \lambda_2 S_2 + \cdots + \lambda_k S_k$$

is a *comparison* only if

$$n_1 \lambda_1 + n_2 \lambda_2 + \cdots + n_3 \lambda_3 = 0 \tag{14}$$

where $n_1, n_2, \cdots n_k$ are the number of scores in groups $1, 2, \cdots k$ respectively. In other words, it is now the weighted sum of the coefficients which must be zero, the weights being the sizes of the groups.

In the same way the sum of squares for any comparison is now given by

$$\frac{c^2}{\sum_{i=1}^{k} n_i \lambda_i^2}$$

the denominator being the similarly weighted sum of the squares of the coefficients.

Finally, the criterion for the orthogonality of two comparisons is that the weighted sum of the products of corresponding coefficients be zero, the weights being the sizes of the groups; i.e. with the same notation as before (p. 63), the comparisons c_1 and c_2 are orthogonal if

$$n_1 \lambda_{11} \lambda_{21} + n_2 \lambda_{12} \lambda_{22} + \cdots + n_k \lambda_{1k} \lambda_{2k} = 0 \tag{15}$$

The sum of squares for each successive comparison, from a set of mutually orthogonal comparisons, is a residual of the between-groups sum in exactly the same way as before.

3.6 Testing for homogeneity of variance

At the end of chapter 2 we mentioned that a suspected lack of homogeneity of variance may be investigated by a test devised by Bartlett (1937). The test will now be described from data set out in table 3.6 (p. 59). We may note that the group variances differ appreciably. Thus, for instance, group 3 is seen to have a range of scores twice that of group 2, and its

Statistical table 3 Distribution of χ^2*

Degrees of freedom	*Probability that the value of χ^2 shown in the body of the table will be exceeded in random sampling*							
	0·90	0·70	0·50	0·30	0·10	0·05	0·02	0·01
1	0·016	0·15	0·46	1·07	2·71	3·84	5·41	6·64
2	0·21	0·71	1·39	2·41	4·60	5·99	7·82	9·21
3	0·58	1·42	2·37	3·66	6·25	7·82	9·84	11·34
4	1·06	2·19	3·36	4·88	7·78	9·49	11·67	13·28
5	1·61	3·00	4·35	6·06	9·24	11·07	13·39	15·09
6	2·20	3·83	5·35	7·23	10·64	12·59	15·03	16·81
7	2·83	4·67	6·35	8·38	12·02	14·07	16·62	18·48
8	3·49	5·53	7·34	9·52	13·36	15·51	18·17	20·09
9	4·17	6·39	8·34	10·66	14·68	16·92	19·68	21·67
10	4·86	7·27	9·34	11·78	15·99	18·31	21·16	23·21
11	5·58	8·15	10·34	12·90	17·28	19·68	22·62	24·72
12	6·30	9·03	11·34	14·01	18·55	21·03	24·05	26·22
13	7·04	9·93	12·34	15·12	19·81	22·36	25·47	27·69
14	7·79	10·82	13·34	16·22	21·06	23·68	26·87	29·14
15	8·55	11·72	14·34	17·32	22·31	25·00	28·26	30·58
16	9·31	12·62	15·34	18·42	23·54	26·30	29·63	32·00
17	10·08	13·53	16·34	19·51	24·77	27·59	31·00	33·41
18	10·86	14·40	17·34	20·60	25·99	28·87	32·35	34·80
19	11·65	15·35	18·34	21·69	27·20	30·14	33·69	36·19
20	12·44	16·27	19·34	22·78	28·41	31·41	35·02	37·57
21	13·24	17·18	20·34	23·86	29·62	32·67	36.34	38·93
22	14·04	18·10	21·34	24·94	30·81	33·92	37·66	40·29
23	14·85	19·02	22·34	26·02	32·01	35·17	38·97	41·64
24	15·66	19·94	23·34	27·10	33·20	36·42	40·27	42·98
25	16·47	20·87	24·34	28·17	34·38	37·65	41·57	44·31
26	17·29	21·79	25·34	29·25	35·56	38·88	42·86	45·64
27	18·11	22·72	26·34	30·32	36·74	40·11	44·14	46.96
28	18·94	23·65	27·34	31·39	37·92	41·34	45·42	48·28
29	19·77	24·58	28·34	32·46	39·09	42·56	46·69	49·59
30	20·60	25·51	29·34	33·53	40·26	43·77	47·96	50·89

* Adapted from table 4 of Fisher, R. A. and Yates, F., *Statistical Tables for Biological, Agricultural and Medical Research*, Oliver & Boyd, 6th edition 1963, by permission of the authors and publishers.

variance is actually more than three times that of group 2. The calculations are set out in table 3.9.

The sums of squares in the first column of the table are the within-groups sums, and their total is the within-groups sum previously obtained (table 3.7). Similarly, the overall within-groups mean square, S_w^2, is the same as that previously obtained. The last two columns involve the logarithms of the separate group mean squares (i.e. the sum of squares divided by the degrees of freedom). The factor 2·3026 in the calculation of χ^2 is necessary because common logarithms are used.

The resulting χ^2 when referred to statistical table 3 with 7 degrees of freedom shows a probability of over 0·70, i.e. it would arise by chance, on the basis of equal population variances, more than 70 per cent of the time. Clearly there is no evidence against the hypothesis of equal population variances; homogeneity of variance may be accepted.

The result in view of the observed differences in group variance is suggestive. Again, even if the test gave a χ^2 significant, at some predetermined level, such as 5 per cent, it would not necessarily mean that the extent of heterogeneity is marked. In fact, the test—unlike the t and F tests of significance—is *not* robust, and is in particular sensitive to lack of normality of distribution. Indeed, if some of the groups came from markedly non-normal populations, a 'significant' result could be obtained even if the population variances were in fact equal. Therefore, in view of the robustness of the F test itself (and especially for the case of groups all of equal size), we might well conclude that Bartlett's test has only a limited value. In fact, Box (1953) has commented that 'to make the preliminary test on variances is rather like putting to sea in a rowing boat to find out whether the conditions are sufficiently calm for an ocean liner to leave port!'

We may conclude, nevertheless, that if in a particular investigation we had some previous indication that the population variances differed (though at the same time no evidence to suggest non-normality), Bartlett's test would still be of value. It would follow, too, that if the suspected heterogeneity of variance was borne out, procedures other than those described in this chapter for testing the significance of differences among the group means would have to be used. Accounts of such procedures are provided by Welch (1947) and Snedecor (1956, pp. 287–9).

References

BARTLETT, M. S. (1937) 'Some examples of statistical methods of research in agriculture and applied biology,' *Journal of the Royal Statistical Society Supplement*, **4**, 137–70.

BOX, G. E. P. (1953) 'Non-normality and tests on variance,' *Biometrika*, **40**, 318–35.

FEDERER, W. T. (1955) *Experimental Design*, New York: Macmillan, pp. 20–4.

KEMPTHORNE, O. (1952) *The Design and Analysis of Experiments*, New York: Wiley, pp. 104–5.

RYAN, T. A. (1959) 'Multiple comparisons in psychological research,' *Psychological Bulletin*, **56**, 26–47.

SCHEFFÉ, H. (1953) 'A method for judging all contrasts in analysis of variance,' *Biometrika*, **40**, 87–104.

SNEDECOR, G. W. (1956) *Statistical Methods*, Iowa State College Press (5th edition).

TUKEY, J. W. (1953) *The Problem of Multiple Comparisons*, Unpublished mimeographed notes, Princeton University.

WELCH, B. L. (1947) 'The generalization of Student's problem when several different population variances are involved,' *Biometrika*, **34**, 28–35.

WILK, M. B. and KEMPTHORNE, O. (1955) 'Fixed, mixed and random models,' *Journal of the American Statistical Association*, **50**, 1144–67.

Chapter 4 Nesting Designs

4.1 Introduction

We now consider designs where the sampling, and hence also the element of randomization, comes in at more than one stage, one set of sampling units being contained or 'nested' within another. Suppose, for instance, that we are investigating how suitable a new apparatus is as a teaching aid in primary-school arithmetic (such as, for example, the Dienes Multibase Blocks in teaching the concept of place value). We would wish, in the first place, to try out the apparatus in a number of schools. Differences between schools are usually considerable—this being due to differences in the socio-economic status of the majority of homes in the catchment area, and to differences in staffing ratios, the provision of auxiliary equipment, and the like. It might well be that the new apparatus would prove more suitable in some schools than in others. Secondly, however, we would wish to know whether different teachers can make use of the apparatus with reasonable success. In other words, we would have to take account of differences between teachers within the schools. We would also, of course, have to take account of differences between pupils by selecting (at random) groups of pupils for each of the teachers—this, as before, being the basic element of randomization in the design.

We would therefore select:

1. A number of primary schools—possibly a random sample of such schools in a given region, though this is not essential. (Thus it might be better deliberately to select schools from contrasting social areas, or schools with a different internal organization, e.g. streamed and unstreamed schools.)
2. A random sample of teachers in each of the schools.
3. Random groups of pupils within each of the schools, each group being allocated to one of the teachers.

Such a design would provide sampling at two distinct stages, one set of sampling units (pupils) being nested within the other (teachers). While it would not be essential to select equal numbers of pupils for each teacher, or equal numbers of teachers for each school, this arrangement is to be preferred in that it provides the most economical use of resources. An experiment designed along these lines will now be described.

4.2 An experiment with two levels of sampling

We will suppose that an investigation into the suitability of a new apparatus as a teaching aid is conducted in four schools, that three teachers are selected at random from each of the schools, and that each teacher uses the apparatus with a random group of six pupils. This implies that, within each school, the teachers selected would have to be allocated at random to the (randomly selected) pupil groups. We will suppose, too, that after a planned series of lessons the attainments of all the pupils on a suitable test are as shown in table 4.1.

The partitioning of the sum of squares will now take account of the differences between schools, and of the differences between teachers within schools. The calculation is as follows:

1. Overall sum of scores, $\sum x = 630+754+697+654 = 2735$

$$\left(\text{The overall mean is therefore } \frac{2735}{72} = 37{\cdot}99\right)$$

2. Correction term (overall), $\dfrac{(\sum x)^2}{N} = \dfrac{2735 \times 2735}{72} = 103{,}892{\cdot}01$

3. Total sum of squares $= (44^2+41^2+\cdots+29^2)$ Sum of 72 terms $-103{,}892{\cdot}01$

$$= 105{,}637{\cdot}00 - 103{,}892{\cdot}01$$
$$= 1{,}744{\cdot}99$$

4. Between-schools sum of squares $= \dfrac{630^2}{18}+\dfrac{754^2}{18}+\dfrac{697^2}{18}+\dfrac{654^2}{18} - 103{,}892{\cdot}01$

Table 4.1 Scores of pupils from three groups in each of four schools

	SCHOOLS											
	I			*II*			*III*			*IV*		
	Teacher			*Teacher*			*Teacher*			*Teacher*		
	1	2	3	1	2	3	1	2	3	1	2	3
	44	39	39	51	48	44	46	45	43	42	45	39
	41	37	36	49	43	43	43	40	41	39	40	38
	39	35	33	45	42	42	41	38	39	38	37	35
	36	35	31	44	40	39	40	38	37	36	37	35
	35	34	28	40	37	37	36	35	34	34	32	35
	32	30	26	40	34	36	34	34	33	31	32	29
Teacher totals	227	210	193	269	244	241	240	230	227	220	223	211
(means)	(37·83)	(35·00)	(32·17)	(44·83)	(40·67)	(40·16)	(40·00)	(38·33)	(37·83)	(36·67)	(37·17)	(35·17)
School totals	630			754			697			654		
(means)	(35·00)			(41·89)			(38·72)			(36·33)		

N.B. There is no connection between the teachers of the different schools. Thus, teacher 1 from school 1 is not the same person as teacher 1 from school 2.

$$= 104{,}385{\cdot}61 - 103{,}892{\cdot}01$$

$$= 493{\cdot}60$$

5. Between-teachers, within-schools sum of squares

$$= \frac{227^2}{6} + \frac{210^2}{6} + \frac{193^2}{6} - \frac{630^2}{18}$$

+ Similar terms for schools II, III and IV

$$= 104{,}589{\cdot}16 - 104{,}385{\cdot}61$$

$$= 203{\cdot}55$$

6. Within-groups sum of squares

$$= 1{,}744{\cdot}99 - 493{\cdot}60 - 203{\cdot}55$$

$$= 1{,}047{\cdot}84$$

As before, the total sum of squares expresses the variation of all the scores without taking account of their separation into groups. It is the sum of the squares of all the scores expressed as deviations from the overall mean (37·99).

The between-schools sum (493·60) expresses only the variation between schools, i.e. the variation that would occur if all the scores were replaced by the mean score of the school to which they belong. It takes no account of the variation between teachers, or of that of individual pupils.

The between-teachers, within-schools sum of squares (203·55) gives a measure of the variation between teachers that results from isolating the teacher differences within each school, and then summing for all schools. Note that the (overall) correction term is *not* now used. Instead we have separate correction terms for each school $\left(\frac{630^2}{18}, \frac{754^2}{18}, \text{etc.}\right)$. The resulting sum is essentially the sum of the squares of all the teacher mean scores expressed as deviations from their own school mean—i.e. $(37{\cdot}83 - 35{\cdot}00)^2$ for the mean score of teacher 1 of school I—increased sixfold (since there are six pupils in each group).

The within-groups sum of squares (1,047·84) obtained above by subtraction could also be described as the sum of squares between pupils within teachers (or groups), and could also be obtained as the sum of the squares of all the scores expressed as deviations from their own group mean (see p. 36).

These sums of squares are set down in table 4.2, together with the corresponding degrees of freedom and mean squares. The degrees of freedom for the variation between teachers within schools are 8, there being 2 degrees of freedom for each set of three teachers in one school. The degrees of freedom for pupils, i.e. within groups, are obtained by subtraction ($71-3-8 = 60$), and also result from the 5 degrees of freedom for a single group multiplied by 12, the number of groups.

Table 4.2 Analysis of variance of the data in table 4.1

Source of variation	*Sum of squares*	*Degrees of freedom*	*Mean square*
Schools (S)	493·60	3	164·53
Teachers (T), within S	203·55	8	25·44
Pupils (P), within T	1,047·84	60	17·46
Total	1,744·99	71	

From table 4.2 we see that the ratio of the mean square for teachers to that for pupils (or within groups) is obtained as $F = \frac{25{\cdot}44}{17{\cdot}46} = 1{\cdot}46$. This is less than the reading in statistical table 2A for 8 and 60 degrees of freedom (2·10). The differences among teachers are not significant at the 5-per-cent level. We may conclude that the new apparatus could be used with equal success by all the teachers.

The significance of the differences between schools is tested not by the mean square for pupils (as above) but by the mean square for teachers. This is because we must incorporate both sources of variation, teachers as well as pupils, in our estimate of statistical error (see also section 4.3). The use of the mean square for pupils as the error term could result in a spuriously high level of significance being claimed for the school differences. For the school differences, therefore, we have $F = \frac{164{\cdot}53}{25{\cdot}44} = 6{\cdot}47$, which exceeds the reading in statistical table 2A for 3 and 8 degrees of freedom (4·07). The school differences are significant at the 5-per-cent level. We may conclude that schools, of the type sampled, would not be equally successful in using the new apparatus as a teaching aid.

4.3 The model

The general model for the breakdown of a single score in the experiment described would be as follows. The score x_{ijk} of the kth pupil in the jth teacher group in the ith school is assumed to consist of four independent components given by

$$x_{ijk} = M+S_i+T_{ij}+e_{ijk} \qquad (16)$$

where M is a component common to all the scores;
S_i is a component common to all scores in school i;
T_{ij} is a component common to all scores in the teacher group j within school i;
and e_{ijk} is a component specific to pupil k of teacher group j within school i.

In the particular experiment described, i would run from 1 to 4, j from 1 to 3 and k from 1 to 6.

We may put S_i equal to the population mean of the scores for school i expressed as a deviation from the mean of the population means for all the schools. In other words, summing for all the schools, $\sum_i S_i = 0$ (see p. 55). As before, we may also put M equal to the mean of the population means for all the schools. Thus, in table 4.1 the overall mean of the seventy-two scores, 37·99, estimates M, $35{\cdot}00-37{\cdot}99 = -2{\cdot}99$ estimates S_1, $41{\cdot}89-37{\cdot}99 = 3{\cdot}90$ estimates S_2, $38{\cdot}72-37{\cdot}99 = 0{\cdot}73$ estimates S_3, and $36{\cdot}33-37{\cdot}99 = -1{\cdot}66$ estimates S_4.

Similarly, we may put T_{ij} equal to the population mean of the scores of teacher group j within school i (i.e. the mean of all the scores that would result if the population had all been taught by this particular teacher in this particular school) and express this as a deviation from the population mean of all the scores for school i (i.e. as a deviation from $M+S_i$). Summing for all the teachers in the school, we therefore have $\sum_j T_{ij} = 0$, and for each i in turn. In table 4.1 $37{\cdot}83-35{\cdot}00 = 2{\cdot}83$ estimates T_{11}, $35{\cdot}00-35{\cdot}00 = 0{\cdot}00$ estimates T_{12}, and so on.

We also assume that for any one school the population means for the different teacher groups themselves form part of a normally distributed population with a variance *which is the same as that for each of the other schools in turn.* We shall denote this common population variance of teacher group means by σ_T^2.

Finally, since e_{ijk} is the specific contribution of a pupil in one teacher group, and since $M+S_i+T_{ij}$ already gives the population mean of the scores for that group, it follows that, summing with respect to k for the whole population, $\sum_k e_{ijk} = 0$. It follows that the mean of all the e_{ijk}s is also zero. We assume, too, that for any given i and j, e_{ijk} is from a normally distributed population, with a variance *which is the same for all such populations*, i.e. for all values of i and j in turn. As before we shall denote this common population variance by σ^2.

Table 4.3 Components analysis for a nesting design

Source of variation	*Degrees of of freedom**	*Mean-square expectation*
Schools (S)	$s-1$	$\sigma^2+n\sigma_T^2+tn\sigma_S^2$
Teachers (T), within S	$s(t-1)$	$\sigma^2+n\sigma_T^2$
Pupils (P), within T	$st(n-1)$	σ^2
Total	$stn-1$	

* These are written for s schools, with t teachers within each school, and with n pupils for each teacher.

In summary, then, we may simply say that the model supposes e_{ijk} to be drawn from a normally distributed population with a mean of zero and a variance of σ^2, while T_{ij} is drawn from a normally distributed population with a mean of zero, and a variance of σ_T^2.

The components analysis may then be written as shown in table 4.3. With n pupils in each of the teacher groups, the mean-square expectation for teachers is $\sigma^2+n\sigma_T^2$ in precisely the same way as that for groups in table 3.5 (p. 58). Similarly, with t teacher groups within each school (and therefore tn pupils within each school), an additional component $tn\sigma_S^2$ appears in the mean-square expectation for schools, σ_S^2 representing the variance of the population of schools of which the particular schools chosen may be considered a random sample. (Alternatively, this component would be written as $\frac{tn\sum_i S_i^2}{s-1}$, s being the number of schools, if the schools effect is to be regarded as fixed; see p. 57.) We note, therefore, that all three components enter into the mean-square expectation for schools, one component for each of the independent sources of variation, pupils, teachers and schools. This must be so, since the obtained differences between schools would obviously be affected by any real differences between the schools themselves and any real differences between the teachers within the schools, as well as by differences between the pupils within the teaching groups.

From table 4.3 it is obvious that the appropriate error term for testing the significance of school differences (i.e. σ_S^2 not being zero) is the mean square for teachers. This is because

$$F = \frac{\text{Mean square for schools}}{\text{Mean square for teachers}} \text{ estimates } \frac{\sigma^2 + n\sigma_T^2 + tn\sigma_S^2}{\sigma^2 + n\sigma_T^2}$$

i.e. a quantity greater than unity only if σ_S^2 is non-zero. In the same way teacher differences are tested by the mean square for pupils, since

$$F = \frac{\text{Mean square for teachers}}{\text{Mean square for pupils}} \text{ estimates } \frac{\sigma^2 + n\sigma_T^2}{\sigma^2}$$

which is greater than unity only if σ_T^2 is non-zero.

Clearly we must always select for our error term the mean square estimating all components in the mean-square expectation of the differences tested except one—the additional component involving the specific effect (schools, teachers, etc.) being tested.

4.4 Modification for a model with fixed effects

The model just described is, of course, one with random effects, both teachers and pupils being randomly selected. Suppose, however, that our interest is not with teacher differences but with method differences, and that in each of the schools concerned the same three methods were used. We could, for instance, eliminate the distinctive influence of particular teachers by programming the different methods, the human teachers being replaced by, say, linear programmes, so that for any one method the same sequence of operations would be covered in all the schools. The comparison of teachers would now be replaced by a comparison of methods, but the methods—unlike the teachers—would not be subject to sampling. They would give rise to fixed effects. The model now having both random effects (for pupils) and fixed effects (for methods) would be described as a *mixed model*, and the components analysis would be as shown in table 4.4.

Table 4.4 Components analysis for the nesting design of table 4.3, with methods replacing teachers

Source of variation	*Degrees of freedom**	*Mean-square expectation*
Schools (S)	$s-1$	$\sigma^2+mn\sigma_S^2$
Methods (M), within S	$s(m-1)$	$\sigma^2+n\sigma_M^2$
Pupils (P), within M	$sm(n-1)$	σ^2
Total	$smn-1$	

* These are written for s schools, with m methods within each school, and n pupils in each method group within each school.

Table 4.4 corresponds to table 4.3, with M (for methods) replacing T (for teachers)—and hence σ_M^2, the population variance of the method means, replacing σ_T^2—and with m (number of methods within each school) replacing t. The mean-square expectation for methods therefore becomes $\sigma^2+n\sigma_M^2$. The mean-square expectation for schools, however, is not $\sigma^2+n\sigma_M^2+mn\sigma_S^2$ but simply $\sigma^2+mn\sigma_S^2$. This is because M is a fixed effect, and differences in methods (which are precisely the same for each of the schools) do *not* contribute to the obtained differences between schools. These differences must now be tested for significance against the mean square for pupils, since

$$F = \frac{\text{Mean square for schools}}{\text{Mean square for pupils}} \text{ estimates } \frac{\sigma^2+mn\sigma_S^2}{\sigma^2}$$

which is greater than unity only if σ_S^2 is non-zero. (Thus, the test for the data of table 4.1 would give $F = \frac{164{\cdot}53}{17{\cdot}46} = 9{\cdot}42$, so showing the differences between schools to be significant at the 1-per-cent level, a higher level of significance than before.) The difference from the preceding situation aptly illustrates that the choice of error term should always be dictated by a prior components analysis, not by any rule of thumb. This will become even more apparent as the discussion proceeds.

4.5 A nesting hierarchy

Nesting need not be confined to two levels: it could be extended indefinitely. Thus, to develop our present illustration, we could begin by contrasting two or more types of school (e.g. comprehensive–tripartite, streamed–unstreamed), or two or more regions in the country, select schools in each of these types or regions, select teachers in the schools, and finally select pupils for each of the teacher groups chosen. We would then have a

Table 4.5 Components analysis for a nesting hierarchy, all effects random

Source of variation	*Degrees of freedom*	*Mean-square expectation*
A	$a-1$	$\sigma^2+n\sigma_D^2+dn\sigma_C^2+cdn\sigma_B^2+bcdn\sigma_A^2$
B, within A	$a(b-1)$	$\sigma^2+n\sigma_D^2+dn\sigma_C^2+cdn\sigma_B^2$
C, within B	$ab(c-1)$	$\sigma^2+n\sigma_D^2+dn\sigma_C^2$
D, within C	$abc(d-1)$	$\sigma^2+n\sigma_D^2$
Individuals, within D	$abcd(n-1)$	σ^2
Total	$abcdn-1$	

hierarchy with three levels, with pupils nested within teacher groups, teachers within schools and schools within types (or regions). We could also extend the hierarchy downwards by administering more than one test to the pupils (an objective test and an essay-type test, say)—or, again, administer the same or a parallel test on a second occasion—and so consider also the differences between tests—or between occasions—within pupils. A numerical illustration of this is given later.

Suppose, then, that in a nesting hierarchy A refers to the uppermost level, and that there are a groups of A; that B refers to the second level, and that there are b groups for each of a groups of A; that C refers to the third level, and that there are c groups of C for each of the ab groups of B; that D refers to the fourth level, and that there are d groups of D for each of the abc groups of C. (We could obviously continue the process indefinitely with levels E, F, G, etc., but the general argument should now be apparent.) With the same notation as before (equation 16, p. 75) the model would be as follows:

$$x_{ijklm} = M + A_i + B_{ij} + C_{ijk} + D_{ijkl} + e_{ijklm} \qquad (17)$$

All five contributions to the score x_{ijklm} would be independent of each other, and the *A*s, *B*s, *C*s, *D*s and *e*s would all be drawn from normally distributed populations with means of zero and variances of σ_A^2, σ_B^2, σ_C^2, σ_D^2 and σ^2 respectively. Also, with *n* individuals in each of the ultimate (*D*) groups, and with all the *A*, *B*, *C* and *D* effects being random, the components analysis would be as shown in table 4.5.

A differences would then be tested for significance against the mean square for *B*; *B* differences against the mean square for *C*; *C* differences against the mean square for *D*; and *D* differences against the mean square for individuals.

Suppose, however, that one of the effects, *C* say, is fixed. This implies that differences arising from *C* are precisely the same (i.e. *not* subject to sampling) for each of the *ab* groups of the higher-level classifications (*A* and *B*), and that σ_C^2—which might also be written as $\frac{\sum C_i^2}{c-1}$ in the third row of table 4.5, there being now no population for the *C*s—does not contribute at all to the variation of *A* and *B*. The term $dn\sigma_C^2$ must, therefore, be deleted from the first two rows of table 4.5, and the mean-square expectations would then be as shown in table 4.6.

The *B* differences would now be tested for significance against the mean square for *D*, not *C*, the *A*, *C* and *D* differences being tested for significance in the same way as before. The reader may easily verify that if, in addition, the *D* effect is fixed, both the *B* and *C* differences would then be tested for significance against the mean square for individuals.

4.6 An experiment with three levels of sampling

A convenient illustration of a three-level nesting hierarchy can be developed from the experiment described in section 4.2. Thus, suppose that having selected the schools, and having sampled teachers within the schools as before, we now decide to test the effectiveness of the new teaching apparatus both immediately after the series of lessons and after an interval of, say, a week. Our intention, in other words, is to test retention as well as immediate learning. We express this by saying that we are sampling *occasions within teachers*, by arranging for each teacher to teach two groups of pupils, one of the groups taking an immediate test (at the conclusion of the teaching)—occasion i—and the other a delayed test—occasion ii. We finally select random groups of pupils for each occasion. To illustrate the partitioning of the total sum of squares, we will suppose that the test scores shown in table 4.7 have been obtained. All the occasion i scores have, in fact, been reproduced from table 4.1.

Table 4.6 Components analysis for the nesting hierarchy of table 4.5, with the *C* effect fixed

Source of variation	*Degrees of freedom*	*Mean-square expectation*
A	$a-1$	$\sigma^2+n\sigma_D^2+cdn\sigma_B^2+bcdn\sigma_A^2$
B, within A	$a(b-1)$	$\sigma^2+n\sigma_D^2+cdn\sigma_B^2$
C, within B	$ab(c-1)$	$\sigma^2+n\sigma_D^2+dn\sigma_C^2$
D, within C	$abc(d-1)$	$\sigma^2+n\sigma_D^2$
Individuals, within D	$abcd(n-1)$	σ^2
Total	$abcdn-1$	

We must now take account of differences between schools, differences between teachers within schools, differences between occasions within teachers as well as the basic differences between pupils (or differences between pupils within occasions) as the ultimate within-groups sum of squares. The calculation is as follows:

1. Overall sum of scores, $\sum x = 1243+1490+1363+1269 = 5365$

2. Correction term (overall), $\dfrac{(\sum x)^2}{N} = \dfrac{5365\times5365}{144} = 199{,}883{\cdot}50$

Table 4.7 Scores of two groups of pupils from each of three teachers in each of four schools, the groups being tested on different occasions

	SCHOOL I						*SCHOOL II*					
	Teacher						*Teacher*					
	1		2		3		1		2		3	
	Occasion i	ii	*Occasion* i	ii	*Occasion* i	ii	*Occasion* i	ii	*Occasion* i	ii	*Occasion* i	ii
	44	42	39	44	39	37	51	47	48	48	44	43
	41	40	37	36	36	36	49	46	43	45	43	40
	39	40	35	35	33	35	45	44	42	44	42	41
	36	35	35	34	31	29	44	42	40	39	39	39
	35	34	34	32	28	24	40	40	37	39	37	35
	32	26	30	32	26	22	40	39	34	35	36	30
Occasion totals	227	217	210	213	193	183	269	258	244	250	241	228
Teacher totals	444		423		376		527		494		469	
Schools totals	1243						1490					

3. Total sum of squares

$$= (44^2+41^2+39^2+\cdots+28^2)$$

Sum of 144 terms

$$-199{,}883{\cdot}50$$

$$= 204{,}127-199{,}883{\cdot}50$$

$$= 4{,}243{\cdot}50$$

4. Between-schools sum of squares

$$= \frac{1243^2}{36}+\frac{1490^2}{36}+\frac{1363^2}{36}+\frac{1269^2}{36}$$

$$-199{,}883{\cdot}50$$

$$= 200{,}924{\cdot}41-199{,}883{\cdot}50$$

$$= 1{,}040{\cdot}91$$

Table 4.7 (continued)

	SCHOOL III						*SCHOOL IV*					
	Teacher						*Teacher*					
	1		2		3		1		2		3	
	Occasion i	ii	*Occasion* i	ii	*Occasion* i	ii	*Occasion* i	ii	*Occasion* i	ii	*Occasion* i	ii
	46	50	45	42	43	41	42	42	45	43	39	40
	43	44	40	40	41	40	39	35	40	40	38	32
	41	41	38	35	39	35	38	35	37	35	35	32
	40	40	38	37	37	32	36	32	37	34	35	30
	36	35	35	36	34	30	34	32	32	33	35	30
	34	32	34	26	33	30	31	32	32	30	29	28
Occasion totals	240	242	230	216	227	208	220	208	223	215	211	192
Teacher totals	482		446		435		428		438		403	
School totals	1363						1269					

5. Between-teachers, within-schools sum of squares

$$= \frac{444^2}{12} + \frac{423^2}{12} + \frac{376^2}{12} - \frac{1243^2}{36}$$

+ Similar terms for schools II, III and IV

$$= 201{,}422{\cdot}41 - 200{,}924{\cdot}41$$

$$= 498{\cdot}00$$

6. Between-occasions, within-teachers sum of squares

$$= \frac{227^2}{6} + \frac{217^2}{6} - \frac{444^2}{12}$$

+ Similar terms for the other 11 teachers

$$= 201{,}561{\cdot}12 - 201{,}422{\cdot}41$$
$$= 138{\cdot}71$$

7. Within-groups sum of squares $= 4{,}243{\cdot}50 - 1{,}040{\cdot}91 - 498{\cdot}00 - 138{\cdot}71$
$$= 2{,}565{\cdot}88$$

The sums of squares for between schools and for between teachers within schools are obtained in the same way as before. The sum for between occasions results from a precisely similar process, using a separate correction term for each occasion $\left(\frac{444^2}{12}, \frac{423^2}{12}, \text{etc.}\right)$ to isolate the occasion differences for each teacher and then to sum for all the teachers. The final within-groups sum, obtained as usual by subtraction, could also have been derived as the sum of squares of the pupils' scores expressed as deviations from their own occasion mean.

The analysis is set down in table 4.8. As before the degrees of freedom for schools and teachers are 3 and 8 respectively. There are 12 degrees of freedom for occasions, 1 for each of the twelve teachers, and $143 - 3 - 8 - 12 = 120$ for pupils (this number also resulting from there being 5 degrees of freedom within each of the twenty-four groups).

Table 4.8 Analysis of variance of the data in table 4.7

Source of variation	*Sum of squares*	*Degrees of freedom*	*Mean square*
Schools (S)	1,040·91	3	346·97
Teachers (T), within S	498·00	8	62·25
Occasions (O), within T	138·71	12	11·56
Pupils (P), within O	2,565·88	120	21·38
Total	4,243·50	143	

The model would now be written with the same notation as before (equation 16, p. 75) as

$$x_{ijkl} = M + S_i + T_{ij} + O_{ijk} + e_{ijkl} \tag{18}$$

x_{ijkl} being the score of the lth pupil in the kth occasion within the jth teacher of the ith school, and where the components M, S_i and T_{ij} are the same as before, where O_{ijk} is the component common to all scores of occasion k within teacher j within school i, and where e_{ijkl} is the component specific to pupil l of occasion k within teacher j within school i. (i runs from 1 to 4, and j from 1 to 3 as before, but k now assumes only the values 1 and 2 and l runs from 1 to 6.) The components analysis would then be as shown in table 4.9, σ_S^2, σ_T^2, σ_O^2 and σ^2 denoting the population variances of the respective components in the same way as before. The occasions (O) effect is fixed—we have not *randomly* selected the two testing occasions, but have selected them deliberately to test immediate and retained learning—so that the term $n\sigma_O^2$ does not appear in the mean-square expectations for teachers and schools.

Table 4.9 Components analysis for a schools–teachers–occasions–pupils nesting hierarchy

Source of variation	*Degrees of freedom**	*Mean-square expectation*
Schools (S)	$(s-1)$	$\sigma^2+on\sigma_T^2+ton\sigma_S^2$
Teachers (T), within S	$s(t-1)$	$\sigma^2+on\sigma_T^2$
Occasions (O), within T	$st(o-1)$	$\sigma^2+n\sigma_O^2$
Pupils (P), within O	$sto(n-1)$	σ^2
Total	$ston-1$	

* These are written for s schools, with t teachers in each school, o occasions for each teacher and n pupils within each occasion.

School differences would then be tested for significance as before against the mean square for teachers, but both teacher and occasion differences would now be tested against the mean square for pupils. From table 4.8, therefore, we have for the school differences $F = \dfrac{346{\cdot}97}{62{\cdot}25} = 5{\cdot}57$, which for 3 and 8 degrees of freedom is significant at the 5-per-cent level (statistical table 2A). For the teacher differences we have $F = \dfrac{62{\cdot}25}{21{\cdot}38} = 2{\cdot}91$, which for 3 and 120 degrees of freedom is significant at the 5-per-cent level (statistical table 2A). Finally, for the occasion differences we have $F = \frac{11 \cdot 56}{21 \cdot 38} < 1$, showing that the differences between occasions are too small for significance at the 5-per-cent level. Indeed, occasion differences of the magnitude shown in table 4.8 could be expected more than half the time from chance. We may conclude that schools would not be equally successful in using the new apparatus; that judged by the total evidence available (and not that from occasion i alone) the apparatus could not be used with equal success by all teachers in the schools; and that whatever success the apparatus has may be taken to apply both to immediate and retained learning.

One feature of the design deserves special note. The two groups selected for each of the teachers must be *independent* random samples. (Mathematically the set of specific components e_{ijkl} for the different values of l must be independent from the sets resulting from the previously taken different values of k—and, for that matter, for the different values of i and j, too.) It would not do for the groups to be matched in any way, still less for the groups to consist of the same pupils tested twice. Yet from the viewpoint of administrative efficiency this would seem the obvious arrangement to make. Why should not all the pupils taught be tested on both occasions? Any disadvantage from memory effects could be removed by using not the same test but a parallel test on the second occasion. The answer is that this arrangement could well be adopted, and would in fact have a decided advantage over using different pupils for the two occasions, but that if it were adopted the mode of analysis just described would be inadequate. It would be inadequate because the partitioning of the total variation has taken no account of the differences between pupils *across occasions*.

Suppose, for instance, that within each of the teacher blocks of table 4.7 the two scores in each row, under occasions i and ii, belong to the same pupil. These scores could then be totalled to give a pupil total, in the same way as the scores in each column have been totalled to give an occasion total, and from which a sum of squares for the differences between pupils within teachers could be derived corresponding to the sum of squares between occasions within teachers already obtained. Indeed, we could then also view the design as one with pupils (not occasions) nested within teachers, and occasions within pupils! A full account of a design of this type is given in chapter 5.

Chapter 5 Crossing Designs: Randomized Blocks

5.1 Introduction

In almost all research involving school pupils, college or university students, and indeed human beings generally, the one outstanding feature found is the very considerable extent of individual variation. This renders the randomized-groups design of little value unless we are able to offset the effect of individual differences by having very large groups. It is usually more economical to seek other ways of combating individual variation. One such way is afforded by the *randomized-blocks* design.

The randomized-blocks design is based on the principle of grouping into blocks persons who are expected to respond to the treatment of the experiment in a broadly similar manner—more similar, at any rate, than would be the case from a completely random group. By taking account of differences between the blocks, and removing these from the usual within-groups variation, a smaller error term—one based solely on differences within the blocks—will be obtained.

The term 'block' derives from experiments in agriculture, where, for example, differences in the effectiveness of various fertilizers or other soil treatments are investigated. The field available for the experiment cannot be expected to be completely uniform. Some parts would be more fertile than others. Blocks are therefore marked out in such a way as to control differences in the natural fertility of the soil. Plots are then marked out in each of the blocks—the number of plots being equal to the number of treatments being investigated—and each treatment allocated at random to one of the plots in every block (see figure 4). In this manner it is hoped that a major portion of the differences in natural soil fertility—a factor extraneous to the experiment—will be apportioned to the differences between blocks, leaving a much reduced portion for the differences within blocks.

In educational experiments concerned with human learning the most obvious measure on which to form blocks is the person's intelligence, or, alternatively, his previous attainment in the type of task being studied. The variation in performance among school pupils all between I.Q. 110 and 120 in a methods experiment, for instance, could be expected to be far less than that among a group selected without regard to intelligence. Comparisons between two or more methods groups would then be more likely to show real differences.* In other experiments appropriate measures on which to form blocks might be the score on a suitable pre-test, socio-economic status, sex, age and, in the non-cognitive field, such traits as extraversion, industriousness and emotional stability. The important consideration is that the persons within the same block should be more alike with respect to their probable response to the treatment than a completely random group. There is no point in forming blocks on the basis of something unrelated to the ability or trait being investigated.

We should note, too, that although the choice of persons for each plot (or treatment subgroup) is restricted by conformity to the block, random selection within the bounds of this restriction is still necessary. The randomized-blocks design may in fact be regarded as embodying a series of randomized-groups experiments, one such experiment for each of the blocks.

5.2 A two-way experiment

For an illustration of a randomized-blocks design we turn to a methods experiment in which pupils are randomly selected for two method groups within each of three I.Q. ranges (for example, I.Q.s 90–99, 100–109 and 110–119). Intelligence, in other words, is the measure used to form the blocks. For convenience of exposition we shall label the three blocks 'superior', 'average' and 'inferior'. With two methods being compared—in the terminology of the agricultural field experiment, two plots within each of three blocks—there will be six pupil groups in all, and so the final test scores may be arranged in the cells of a 2×3 table, as shown in table 5.1. Generally it would be better to select equal numbers in each group. The analysis to be described, however, also permits the group numbers in any pair of rows or columns to be proportionate, i.e. for any two rows (or

* Methods groups so selected are described as 'matched' groups—matched with respect to intelligence in this instance—and hence the randomized-blocks design may also be described as a matched-groups design.

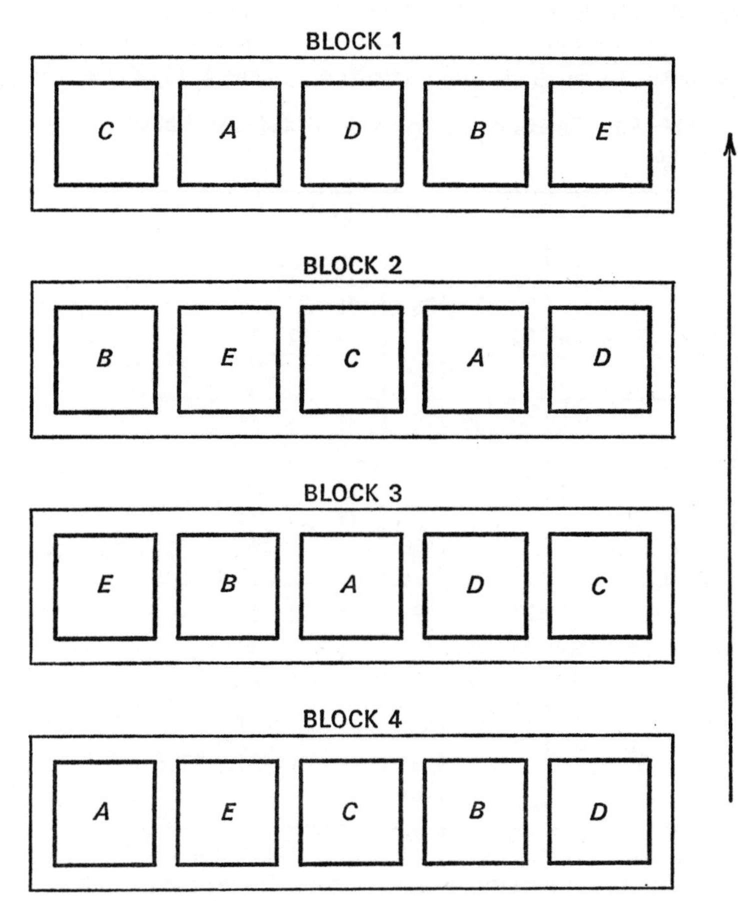

Figure 4 Field plan of a randomized-blocks experiment with five treatments (*A*, *B*, *C*, *D* and *E*).

columns) the numbers in each column (or row) must be in the same proportion throughout. This more general case is now taken, with the group numbers for methods 1 and 2 being 4, 8, 6 and 6, 12, 9 respectively.

Table 5.1 Scores of six groups in a randomized-blocks design

		Methods (*A*)		
		1	2	Totals
	Superior	36 33 28 23 120	41 35 34 34 32 29 205	325 (10)
I.Q. levels (*B*)	Average	30 27 26 25 25 24 21 20 198	35 34 33 32 32 30 30 29 28 27 25 24 359	557 (20)
	Inferior	27 25 23 22 20 18 135	28 23 22 21 21 20 20 18 16 189	324 (15)
	Totals	453 (18)	753 (27)	1206 (45)

N.B. The total score of each cell is shown circled. The number of scores contributing to each of the method and level totals is shown in parentheses.

Each of the forty-five test scores can be classified in two ways, as belonging to a particular method (*A*) and also to a particular block or I.Q. level (*B*). Our interest, of course, is in the difference between methods within each of the levels as well as how these differences themselves differ from level to level. It is best to extract systematically from the total variance the differences between levels (rows in table 5.1) as well as the differences between methods (columns) in the manner already described (chapter 3).

We begin, however, by separating the total variation into the differences between cells—the scores of one method at any level being grouped into one of the six cells of table 5.1—without taking account of the twofold classification of these cells, and the differences within cells. Differences between cells are then analysed into components expressing the differences due solely to (a) methods, (b) levels, and (c) a remainder, a component which is termed the *interaction* between methods and levels. The complete partitioning is shown in figure 5.

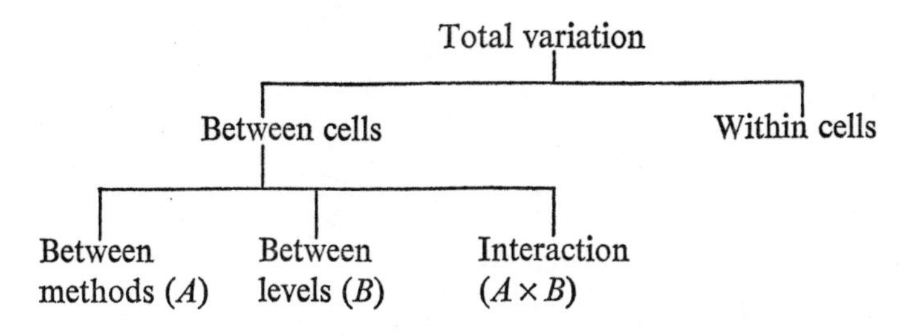

Figure 5 Breakdown of variation in a two-way methods experiment

The calculation is as follows:

1. Total sum of squares $= \underbrace{(36^2+33^2+\cdots+16^2)}_{\text{Sum of 45 terms}} - \dfrac{1206 \times 1206}{45}$

$= 33{,}776 - 32{,}320{\cdot}80$

$= 1{,}455{\cdot}20$

2. Between-cells sums of squares $= \underbrace{\left(\dfrac{120^2}{4} + \dfrac{205^2}{6} + \cdots + \dfrac{189^2}{9}\right)^*}_{\text{Sum of 6 terms}} - \dfrac{1206^2}{45}$

$= 33{,}251{\cdot}25 - 32{,}320{\cdot}80$

$= 930{\cdot}45$

3. Within-cells sum of squares $= 1{,}455{\cdot}20 - 930{\cdot}45$

$= 524{\cdot}75$

(This completes the initial separation of the total variation into between and within cells; the subsequent partitioning of the variation between cells is as shown below.)

* See p. 42.

4. Between-methods (A) sum of squares $= \dfrac{453^2}{18} + \dfrac{753^2}{27} - \dfrac{1206^2}{45}$

$= 32{,}400{\cdot}83 - 32{,}320{\cdot}80$

$= 80{\cdot}03$

5. Between-levels (B) sum of squares $= \dfrac{320^2}{10} + \dfrac{557^2}{20} + \dfrac{324^2}{15} - \dfrac{1206^2}{45}$

$= 33{,}073{\cdot}35 - 32{,}320{\cdot}80$

$= 752{\cdot}55$

6. Interaction ($A \times B$) sum of squares $= 930{\cdot}45 - 80{\cdot}03 - 752{\cdot}55$

$= 97{\cdot}87$

Table 5.2 Mean scores from table 5.1

		Cell means		*Level means*	*Difference in method means*
		Methods (A)			
		1	2		(2–1)
	Superior	30·00	34·17	32·50	4·17
Levels (B)	Average	24·75	29·92	27·85	5·17
	Inferior	22·50	21·00	21·60	−1·50
Method means		25·17	27·89	Overall mean = 26·80	

The between-cells sum of squares measures the variation that would remain if all the differences among pupils of the same method and level were removed, i.e. if each score in table 5.1 were replaced by the mean score of the cell to which it belongs. It is the same as the sum of the squares of each cell mean expressed as a deviation from the overall mean (see table 5.2) and multiplied by the number of scores in the cell, i.e. $(30{\cdot}00 - 26{\cdot}80)^2 \times 4$, plus similar terms for the other cells. Since there are six cells in all, the sum has 5 degrees of freedom.

The between-methods sum of squares accounts solely for differences between the two method means. It measures the variation that would exist if each score were replaced by the mean score of the method to which it belongs. Since there are only two methods, this sum has 1 degree of freedom.

In the same way, the between-levels sum takes account of the differences between the three level means, measuring the variation that would exist if each score were replaced by the mean of the level to which it belongs. There are three levels, so the degrees of freedom are now 2.

The salient feature is that these last two sums do not fully account for the between-cells sum of squares. A residual exists, the methods × levels (read 'methods *by* levels') interaction. This is a measure of the extent to which the method differences for each of the three levels *differ among themselves*. Thus, from table 5.2 we see that at both the superior and average levels method 2 is the more effective (mean differences 4·17 and 5·17 respectively), whereas at the inferior level it is method 1 which is the more effective (mean difference −1·50). It is the interaction sum of squares which takes account of the differences among these three mean differences. If, by some fluke, one method was found to be the more effective at all three levels and *to precisely the same extent*, the interaction sum would be zero. Since the between-cells sum of squares has 5 degrees of freedom, and 1 and 2 of these are accounted for by the between-methods and the between-levels sums respectively, the interaction sum must have $5-1-2 = 2$ degrees of freedom.

The sums of squares and degrees of freedom for the four independent sources of variation, methods, levels, methods × levels interaction and within cells are set out in table 5.3. The mean square for methods, methods × levels interaction and within cells is also shown. The ratio of the mean square for interaction to that for within cells is obtained as

$$F = \frac{48{\cdot}93}{13{\cdot}27} = 3{\cdot}69$$

which, for 2 and 39 degrees of freedom, is significant at the 5-per-cent level (statistical table 2A). We may conclude that there are real differences in the relative effectiveness of the methods at the different levels.

As a significant interaction has been established, there is really little point in testing the significance of the method differences, though even so it is often done as a matter of routine. Thus, testing the mean square for methods against that for within cells (see section 5.3) we would have

$$F = \frac{80{\cdot}03}{13{\cdot}27} = 6{\cdot}03$$

which for 1 and 39 degrees of freedom is significant at the 5-per-cent level. To conclude that there is a real difference in the effectiveness of the methods, and that method 2 is the more effective (from the method means of table 5.2) would, however, be very misleading. Because of the significance of the interaction, no general statement about the effectiveness of the methods (i.e. one valid for *all* levels) can be made. As is apparent from table 5.2, method 2 is the more effective only for the superior and average levels.

Table 5.3 Analysis of variance of the data in table 5.1

Source of variation	*Sum of squares*	*Degrees of freedom*	*Mean square*
Methods (A)	80·03	1	80·03
Levels (B)	752·55	2	
Interaction, $A \times B$	97·87	2	48·93
Within cells	524·75	39	13·27
Total	1,455·20	44	

It may seem reasonable to conclude, too, that the significance of the interaction results solely from the differences between the inferior level and the other two levels, i.e. there would not be a significant interaction if only the superior and average levels were considered. But this conclusion would not be justified. A methods × levels interaction confined to only two levels should be tested in a separate experiment designed for this purpose.

No test of the significance of the level differences is required, since the different levels were brought into the experiment for the sole purpose of reducing the mean square for error. We have no interest in the level differences as such. If no account had been taken of levels, and if all scores in each method had been obtained from a random sample of pupils from the total ability range, the level sum of squares (752·55) together with the interaction sum (97·87) would have been added to the within-cells sum

(524·75) to give the error sum of squares, i.e. the within-groups sum of a simple randomized-groups design. This error sum would have had $2+2+39 = 43$ degrees of freedom. The loss of 4 degrees of freedom due to the separation of levels is more than offset by the very large reduction in the sum of squares.

We can now appreciate an essential feature of all experimental designs, namely that any reduction in statistical error through the control of an extraneous source of variation—intelligence, in this particular illustration—must be accompanied by a corresponding reduction in the estimate of error. If, in fact, the errors from an extraneous source of variance cannot be removed from the estimate of error, then it would be wrong to control this source of variation in the first place. Suppose, for instance, that in our agricultural field experiment (section 5.1) we discovered an extraneous source of variation other than that of soil fertility, that the right-hand side of the field (figure 4), say, was less favoured than the left-hand by being in the shadow of a building for part of the day. Now in the randomized arrangements of plots shown, three of the four plots for treatment *D* would then be on this less favoured side of the field. Why not, then, equalize as far as possible the position of the plots of each treatment with respect to this? (And, incidentally, if we had five blocks instead of four, the equalization could be made complete, see chapter 8.) This argument, though superficially plausible, must be rejected if we are to retain the particular design described. It is imperative that randomization within the blocks play an unfettered role.

Similarly, in our educational illustration, where I.Q. replaces natural soil fertility as the controlled measure, it would not do to match pupils in the different method groups within each level with respect to industriousness, or introversion, or the socio-economic status of the home in an endeavour (which might well be successful) to reduce statistical error still further from the test results. A random selection within each level, and for each method independently, is essential. The discussion of this issue provided by Fisher (1951) cannot be bettered.

5.3 The model

Each score is now regarded as including a part characteristic of the particular method to which it belongs, a part characteristic of the particular level, and a part resulting from the interaction of the particular method and level. We therefore write the model in the same notation as before (sections 3.3, 4.3 and 4.6) as

$$x_{ijk} = M + A_i + B_j + (AB)_{ij} + e_{ijk}$$

where M is a component common to all the scores;
A_i is a component common to all the scores of method i;
B_j is a component common to all the scores of level j;
$(AB)_{ij}$ is a component resulting from the interaction of method i and level j;
and e_{ijk} is a component specific to pupil k of method i and level j.
Generally i would run from 1 to a, the number of treatments, and j would run from 1 to b, the number of levels (in the particular experiment described $a = 2$ and $b = 3$). If there were an equal number of scores n in each cell, then k would run from 1 to n. If, however, the cell numbers are not equal but proportionate, we would have k running from 1 to n_{ij}, the n_{ij}s being subject to the conditions of proportionality, i.e. the ratio $\frac{n_{ij}}{n_{ij'}}$, being constant for all values of i, j and j' ($\neq j$) being fixed, and the ratio $\frac{n_{ij}}{n_{i'j}}$ being constant for all values of j, i and i' ($\neq i$) being fixed. All five contributions to the score x_{ijk} would be independent of each other, and the As, Bs, (AB)s and es would be regarded as drawn from normally distributed populations with means of zero and variances of σ_A^2, σ_B^2, σ_{AB}^2 and σ^2 respectively. (If A and B are fixed effects—as, in fact, they are in the experiment of section 5.2—then σ_A^2, σ_B^2 and σ_{AB}^2 must be regarded only as alternative symbols for $\frac{\sum_i A_i^2}{a-1}$, $\frac{\sum_j B_j^2}{b-1}$ and $\frac{\sum_i \sum_j (AB)_{ij}^2}{(a-1)(b-1)}$ respectively; see p. 58.)

The restriction that the interaction components have a zero mean needs to be restated in the form that the mean—and hence also the sum—of the $(AB)_{ij}$s should be zero separately for all values of i (summing with respect to j) and also for all values of j (summing with respect to i). In terms of a rectangular arrangement of cells such as that of table 5.1, the interaction components must sum to zero in every row and in every column. The precise nature of interaction may, in fact, best be appreciated if a table is constructed with, say, three methods and three levels, table 5.4.

Table 5.4 A constructed table to illustrate interaction

		Methods (A) 1	2	3	Level totals	Level means
		5	5	5		
		1	2	−3		
		4	4	4		
		6	1	−7		
	1	16	12	−1	27	9
		5	5	5		
		1	2	−3		
		0	0	0		
		−4	1	3		
Levels (B)	2	2	8	5	15	5
		5	5	5		
		1	2	−3		
		−4	−4	−4		
		−2	−2	4		
	3	0	1	2	3	1
Method totals		18	21	6	45	Overall mean
Method means		6	7	2		= 5

Let us put the overall mean M equal to 5, and the population means of the methods A_1, A_2 and A_3 equal to 1, 2 and −3 respectively (so expressing them as deviations from M). The population means of the levels, B_1, B_2 and B_3, we will similarly put equal to 4, 0 and −4. In each cell of the table M is entered first, then the method component A (which is the same for all the cells in any one column), then the level component B (which is the same for all the cells in any one row). Finally components representing possible interactions are added. These could be any numbers whatsoever,

provided that they sum to zero in every row and every column. We ca
therefore fill in only four of these components as we please, the remainin
ones being then determined by the zero sums. This is why the degrees o
freedom for interaction in such a table would be 4, and similarly why the
were only 2 for table 5.1. Generally, with a methods and b levels, th
degrees of freedom will be given by the product of the degrees of freedon
for methods and levels separately, namely $(a-1)(b-1)$.

A point worthy of special note is that the differences in methods ar
unaffected by the level components (the method means in table 5.4 sti
have the postulated deviations of 1, 2 and -3 from the overall mean of 5
and, in the same way, the differences in levels are unaffected by the metho
components. In other words, the effects of methods and levels act indepen
dently of each other.

But although they are independent, the methods and levels effects ar
not additive. Thus, to cite but one instance, method 2 overall is superio
to method 1, and level 1 superior to level 2, yet the most favourabl
combination is not, as might be expected, method 2 acting at level 1. It i
this lack of additivity—the failure of methods and levels in combinatio
to determine the resultant effect at each cross-classification—which is th
essence of interaction. Because of interaction, an overall differenc
between methods (or levels) is not preserved at each level (or for eac
method). The overall difference may well give quite a misleading indicatio
of the separate differences.

Similarly, the magnitude of the interaction is the extent of the failur
of the sums of squares for methods and levels to equal the total sum o
squares. In table 5.4 the sum of squares for methods is given b
$[1^2+2^2+(-3)^2]\times 3 = 42$, and that for levels by $[4^2+0^2+(-4)^2]\times 3 = 96$
These contribute to, but do not equal, the total sum of squares, which i
$(16-5)^2+(12-5)^2+(-1-5)^2+\cdots+(2-5)^2 = 274$. The amount re
maining is the measure of the interaction, a sum that could be obtaine
directly from first principles as $6^2+1^2+(-7)^2+\cdots+4^2 = 136$.

The components analysis is shown in table 5.5, the appropriate mean
square expectations appearing in column 1. An equal number of scores, n
in each cross-classification of methods (A) and levels (B) is assumed. (Th
difference for the case of unequal, but proportionate, group numbers i
that it is replaced by the effective group size calculated in a similar manne
to that described in section 3.4.) The mean-square expectation for inter
action appears as $\sigma^2+n\sigma^2_{AB}$, this following in precisely the same way as th

mean-square expectation for groups in the basic randomized-groups design, table 3.5. Again, with bn scores within each method, $bn\sigma_A^2$ appears in the mean-square expectation for methods, and similarly $an\sigma_B^2$ in the mean-square expectation for levels. In neither case does the component $n\sigma_{AB}^2$ appear. This is because both methods and levels are fixed effects, and so no sampling variation from the cross-classifications as such can be expected. (If the experiment were repeated with different pupils, the interaction components $(AB)_{ij}$ would be precisely the same.)

Table 5.5 Components analysis for a two-factor experiment

Source of variation	Degrees of freedom*	Mean-square expectation		
		1 *A and B fixed*	2 *A fixed, B random*	3 *A and B random*
A	$a-1$	$\sigma^2+bn\sigma_A^2$	$\sigma^2+n\sigma_{AB}^2+bn\sigma_A^2$	$\sigma^2+n\sigma_{AB}^2+bn\sigma_A^2$
B	$b-1$	$\sigma^2+an\sigma_B^2$	$\sigma^2+an\sigma_B^2$	$\sigma^2+n\sigma_{AB}^2+an\sigma_B^2$
$A\times B$	$(a-1)(b-1)$	$\sigma^2+n\sigma_{AB}^2$	$\sigma^2+n\sigma_{AB}^2$	$\sigma^2+n\sigma_{AB}^2$
Within cells	$ab(n-1)$	σ^2	σ^2	σ^2

* These are written for a levels of A and b levels of B.

In contrast, suppose that one of the effects, B say, is random. This, of course, would no longer be a randomized-blocks design, but could, for instance, be a comparison of methods (A) in a number of randomly selected schools (B). The component σ_{AB}^2 would then appear in the mean-square expectation for the fixed effect, A, because differences in A measured across the different categories of B would be subject to sampling variation from the cross-classifications. On the other hand, $n\sigma_{AB}^2$ would not appear in the mean-square expectation for the random effect, B, since differences in B are measured over the A categories which are constant, i.e. they would be precisely the same if the experiment were repeated. In such an experiment, therefore, the mean square for methods would have to be tested for significance against the mean square for interaction as the error term, not against the mean square for within cells.

For the sake of completeness the mean-square expectations when both A and B are random effects are included in table 5.5, though such a case would hardly ever arise in educational research. A full discussion of the design when all the effects, whether fixed or random, are important in their own right is postponed until chapter 6, together with the statement of a rule for writing down the mean-square expectations. Such designs are termed *factorial designs*, and the separate effects, such as A and B, *factors*. It is for this reason that table 5.5 has been described as giving the components analysis for a two-factor experiment.

5.4 Unequal and disproportionate cell numbers

Sometimes, through no fault of the investigator, equal or proportionate numbers of scores in various subgroups or cells are not obtained. In a methods experiment, for instance, one or more pupils may become ill during the course of the experiment, or may be unable to take the final test for some other reason. The result would then be a disproportion in the subgroup numbers. The partitioning of the total sum of squares cannot proceed until this disproportion has been corrected.

One way would be to allow for this possibility from the beginning, and to include in each subgroup slightly more pupils than would finally be needed. Exact equality or proportionality could be attained afterwards by randomly rejecting scores from the unduly large subgroups. If only a few scores have to be rejected, this might be the most sensible method to adopt. But if a large number of scores have to be rejected, it can be criticized as being wasteful, i.e. involving an appreciable sacrifice of data.

With only one or two 'missing' scores the best procedure, therefore, might be to replace each missing score by the *mean* of all the obtained scores in the particular cell or subgroup to which it belongs. It would then be necessary to subtract 1 degree of freedom for each of the scores replaced in this way from the degrees of freedom for *within cells*, and also for *total*. (This would leave unaffected the degrees of freedom for treatments, levels and interaction.) The calculation of the various sums of squares would then proceed in the usual way. The tests of significance would only be approximate, but if only one or two scores have to be replaced, the tests would be sufficiently accurate for most purposes.

Another, slightly more refined, method of dealing with disproportionate subgroup numbers is described by Fei Tsao (1946); it involves adjusting the sums of squares of the scores from all cells, not merely those from cells in which the missing scores occur. The method is applicable when the subgroup numbers differ only slightly from proportionality. For methods of dealing with subgroup numbers differing markedly from proportionality the reader is referred to Snedecor (1956).

5.5 The case of one score per cell

Occasionally a design with just one score per cell is useful. This in terms of figure 4 means that each plot within a block corresponds to an individual, a complete block corresponding to a group of individuals (one for each treatment) matched with respect to the measure forming the blocks. These individuals may, for instance, have equal I.Q.s, or equal scores on a suitable pre-test, and they would be allocated at random to the different treatments in the same way as before. The partitioning of the total sum of squares would then be exactly the same as that of the between-cells sum of squares described in section 5.2 (see figure 5). There is now no variation within cells, since two or more scores per cell would be needed for this, and so no estimate of the population variance σ^2 is possible. The method of calculating the sums of squares for treatments (or methods) and blocks (or levels) would remain as described, and the interaction sum of squares would be obtained once again as a residual by subtraction.

As the blocks would now be groups of matched individuals, it is usually reasonable to regard this effect as random rather than fixed. (Thus, to begin by deciding on certain fixed I.Q.s, and then selecting pupils for these specified I.Q.s would be rather far-fetched. More usual would be the practice of taking a random group and then selecting others for individual matching.) The components analysis would then follow from table 5.5 column 2. With $n = 1$, the mean-square expectations for the three sources of variation would be as follows:

Treatments, A: $\sigma^2+\sigma_{AB}^2+b\sigma_A^2$
Blocks, B: $\sigma^2+a\sigma_B^2$
Interaction, AB: $\sigma^2+\sigma_{AB}^2$

The mean square for treatments would then be tested for significance against that for interaction. No test for blocks is possible; but this would be only of academic interest anyway, as real differences among a random group of individuals may be assumed. Again, no test for interaction is possible, though again real individual × treatment interactions may usually be assumed. The fact that σ^2 by itself is not estimable may therefore be of little consequence.

If, on the other hand, the blocks effect together with that of treatments is fixed, no test of significance is possible at all—as may be seen from table 5.5 column 1. This means that the component σ^2_{AB} must be deleted from the mean-square expectation for treatment as written above. Only if we make an *a priori* assumption of zero interaction (a very questionable step) can the interaction mean square be used as the error term for testing the treatment differences. Of course, if the ratio of the mean square for treatments to that for interaction did exceed the appropriate F ratio in statistical table 2, significance for the treatment differences could safely be claimed. The procedure, however, would too often lead to a false acceptance of the null hypothesis, a failure to detect real treatment differences. The use of a randomized-blocks design with one score per cell for a fixed-effects model should therefore be avoided.

A further illustration of the case of one score per cell is when the same person undergoes all the treatments. This, of course, is only practicable if the treatments do not influence each other (which is hardly ever the case in educational investigations),* or if the influence of previous treatments is itself being investigated. The second situation would arise, for instance, if the treatments consisted of giving the same test—or equivalent forms of the same test, the forms having been equated for difficulty—to a group of pupils, the purpose of the experiment being to study the effect of practice. Each pupil then takes all the treatments and thus corresponds not to a plot but to an entire block of an agricultural field experiment. If, however, equivalent forms of the test provide the different treatments, and these forms have not been equated for difficulty, it would be necessary to adjust systematically the order in which the forms are being administered, so that all do not take form 2 (say) after form 1, and form 3 after form 2. This would introduce another dimension into the design—making it no longer a design with randomized blocks, in fact. A discussion of this is resumed later (chapter 8).

Finally, it may have occurred to the reader that data from experiments such as that described in section 5.2 could also be analysed on the basis of one score per cell by considering only the mean score of each cross-classification. Thus, if a methods experiment were conducted in several

* For example, the same pupil could hardly be taught the same topic by more than one method.

randomly selected schools, the mean score for each method group in each school could provide the data for analysis. The mean square for methods would then be tested for significance against the mean square for interaction as before. Practical advantages would be that the method group sizes do not have to be equal, or proportionate—the analysis would assume that groups of the same size would have produced the same set of mean scores—and the method groups need not be randomly selected within the schools. Again homogeneity of variance need not be assumed within the method groups, an assumption which Lindquist (1940) argues is often not fully justified in method experiments anyhow. If, then, our interest is centred on the overall method differences, an analysis based only on mean scores might have much to recommend it. The main drawback is that no test for the significance of interaction would be possible, so that the proper interpretation of the method differences (even if they are statistically significant) may not be possible. On balance the full analysis is to be preferred.

5.6 A test for non-additivity

Basic to all analyses of variance is the assumption of additivity, i.e. that all the components into which a test score is resolved *add together* to give the obtained result. Components do not necessarily have to be combined in this way. They could, for instance, be combined multiplicatively, the obtained score being the product of the separate components. Tukey (1949) has developed a test of significance for non-additivity, a test which, if satisfied at some predetermined level (such as the 5-per-cent level), would lead to the conclusion that additivity is not a reasonable assumption. The test is illustrated from data shown in table 5.6. Scores for two treatments and eight blocks are shown, together with mean scores for all treatments and blocks and the deviations of these mean scores from the overall mean.

A sum of products is calculated by multiplying each test score by the deviation recorded in its row (or column) and then summing for all scores in the column (or row). Thus, if we decide to multiply by the column deviations $-0{\cdot}75$ and $0{\cdot}75$, the scores in each row would sum to the value shown in column 1 of table 5.7. Thus, for example, the first value in this column is obtained as

$$25\times(-0{\cdot}75)+28\times(0{\cdot}75) = 2{\cdot}25$$

These are then multiplied by the *other* set of deviations—the row deviations in this case—set out again for convenience in column 2 of table 5.7. The products are seen to sum to 15·00. The reader may verify that if we begin by multiplying each test score by the row deviation and sum for each column, and then multiply the values so obtained by the column deviations, the same sum of products will result.

Table 5.6 Test scores for a design with two treatments and eight blocks

	Blocks	*Treatment* *X*	*Y*	*Block sum*	*Block mean*	*Deviation from overall mean*
	1	25	28	53	26·5	7·00
	2	24	25	49	24·5	5·00
	3	22	26	48	24·0	4·50
	4	19	17	36	18·0	−1·50
	5	17	18	35	17·5	−2·00
	6	16	16	32	16·0	−3·50
	7	15	17	32	16·0	−3·50
	8	12	15	27	13·5	−6·00
Treatment sum		150	162	Overall sum = 312		Overall mean = 19·5
Treatment mean		18·75	20·25			
Deviation from overall mean		−0·75	0·75			

Sums of squares are calculated for the row and column deviations. In this example, therefore, we have

$$7{\cdot}00^2+5{\cdot}00^2+\cdots+(-6{\cdot}00)^2 = 161{\cdot}00$$

for the sum of squares of the row deviations, and

$$(-0{\cdot}75)^2+(0{\cdot}75)^2 = 1{\cdot}125$$

for the sum of squares of the column deviations. The sum of squares for non-additivity is then obtained as the square of the sum of products divided by both sums of squares; i.e. in this example it is

Table 5.7 Calculations for a test of non-additivity (from the data of table 5.6)

Weighted sum of row scores 1	*Row deviations* 2	*Products* 1 × 2
2·25	7·00	15·75
0·75	5·00	3·75
3·00	4·50	13·50
−1·50	−1·50	2·25
0·75	−2·00	−1·50
0·00	−3·50	0·00
1·50	−3·50	−5·25
2·25	−6·00	−13·50
	Sum of products =	15·00

Table 5.8 Testing the significance of non-additivity (from the data of table 5.6)

Source of variation	*Sum of squares*	*Degrees of freedom*	*Mean square*
Non-additivity	1·24	1	1·24
Remainder	11·76	6	1·96
Treatment × blocks interaction	13·00	7	

$$\frac{(15{\cdot}00)^2}{161{\cdot}00 \times 1{\cdot}125} = 1{\cdot}24$$

This sum is part of the interaction (treatment × blocks) sum of squares, and has 1 degree of freedom. The reader may verify that the interaction sum of squares for the data of table 5.6 works out as 13·00.* Subtracting

* The total sum of squares is 344·00; the treatment sum is 9·00 and the block sum 322·00, so giving the interaction sum as 344·00 − 9·00 − 322·00 = 13·00.

the sum of squares for non-additivity from this gives a *remainder* sum of 11·76, with 6 degrees of freedom (see table 5.8). It is this which provides the error term for testing the significance of non-additivity.

From table 5.8 $F = \frac{1{\cdot}24}{1{\cdot}96} < 1$, which shows that the effect of non-additivity is far too small for statistical significance. In other words, there is no evidence against additivity for the data of table 5.6.

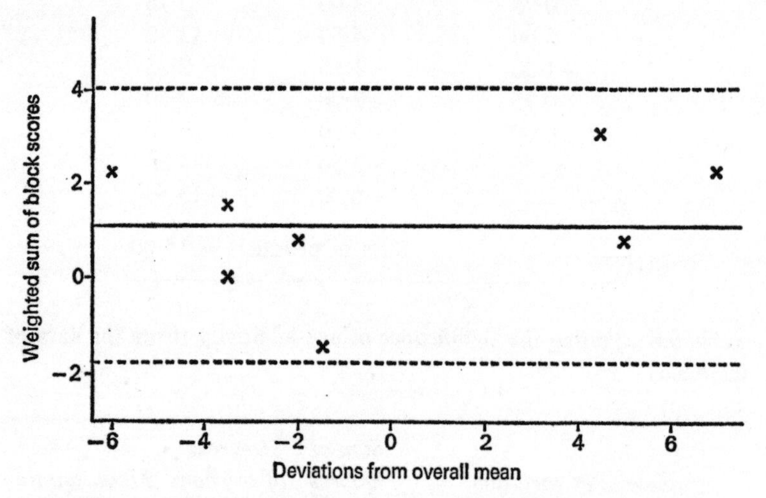

Figure 6 Plot of the weighted sums of block scores against the block deviations from the overall mean (columns 1 and 2 of table 5.7). The unbroken line is the mean of the weighted sums, and the broken lines are confidence limits on each side of the mean.

If the F ratio had shown a significant non-additivity, a possible solution would have been to transform the scale of measurement—though an examination of the data for possible 'discrepant' scores is recommended first. Such an examination would consist of plotting the weighted sum of the row scores (column 1 of table 5.7) against the row deviations (column 2 of table 5.7). These are shown in figure 6. The mean of the weighted sum of row scores is also shown, together with limits set above and below this mean at a distance equal to

$$2\sqrt{(\text{Sum of squares of the treatment deviations}) \times (\text{Remainder mean square})}$$

(In this illustration this distance would be $2\sqrt{1{\cdot}125 \times 1{\cdot}96} = 2{\cdot}92$.) A 'discrepant' score would be revealed by a point in the figure unusually high or low, i.e. outside the limits indicated by the broken lines. A transformation of the scale would be indicated if the points tended to lie on a straight line. The reader is referred to Tukey (1949) for further information.

References

FEI TSAO (1946) 'General solution of the analysis of variance and covariance in the case of unequal or disproportionate numbers of observations in the subclasses,' *Psychometrika*, **2**, 107–28.

FISHER, R. A. (1951) *The Design of Experiments*, Edinburgh: Oliver & Boyd (6th edition), pp. 62–4.

LINDQUIST, E. F. (1940) *Statistical Analysis in Educational Research*, Boston, Mass.: Houghton Mifflin, pp. 132–44.

SNEDECOR, G. W. (1956) *Statistical Methods*, Iowa State College Press (5th edition), pp. 379–87.

TUKEY, J. W. (1949) 'One degree of freedom for non-additivity,' *Biometrics*, **5**, 232–42.

Chapter 6 Crossing Designs: Factorial Arrangements

6.1 Introduction

In chapter 5 a two-way experiment was described in which the effect of blocks was separated from that of treatments in order to reduce statistical error. Different blocks were introduced, in fact, solely for this purpose. Sometimes, however, our interest would be equally divided between the two effects. We might have two distinct sets of treatments, for example—treatments *A* being, say, particular methods in which a topic in a school subject is taught, and treatments *B* the ways in which the groups taught are subsequently examined (e.g. by essay-writing, objective tests, oral questioning). Each set of treatments would then be called *a factor*, and the experimental design a *factorial design.*

A factorial design need not be limited to two factors. Any number of factors can be incorporated. The essential feature is that each factor is investigated in all the combinations of the other factors. A design with three factors is described in section 6.2. The randomized-blocks design of chapter 5 would correspond to a factorial design with two factors. It would be unusual to describe the design in this way because we would have little interest in the effect of the blocks as such.

Possible factors in educational investigations would be methods of teaching, methods of testing, occasions and conditions of testing, grades of intelligence of the testees, and the motivational and personality characteristics of the testees. The classifications based on each of the factors are termed *levels.* With below-average, average and above-average classifications for I.Q., for instance, the factor of intelligence would be said to have three levels. Levels, however, need not be 'ordered', i.e. capable of being quantified: a possible factor in an investigation of reading ability, say, could be the style of type of the reading material used (roman, gothic, clarendon, etc.), each particular style of type then being referred to as a level of the factor of style. All the factors of a factorial design have two or more levels, and the complete arrangement is described by their product. Thus, a $2 \times 3 \times 4$ design would refer to an experiment with three factors, one being investigated at two levels, one at three, and one at four.

It is instructive to contrast the factorial experiment with the one-time 'ideal' of scientific experiment, that of varying the different factors or conditions *one at a time* (see Fisher 1951). The factorial experiment not only provides all the information possible from the separate one-factor-varied experiments (and, moreover, does so more efficiently); it also provides information about the interaction of the factors. This is an important advantage, in that knowing only the effect of a factor with all the others held constant provides no indication at all of whether this effect remains the same at all levels of the other factors. When the number of factors is three or more, there is more than the single interaction of the type already described (section 5.2). The partitioning of the sum of squares becomes complex. A three-factor experiment will therefore be described in some detail, and the extension to experiments with more than three factors may then be readily understood.

6.2 A three-factor experiment

An investigator believes that children will perform differently on a certain task according to various personality traits (in particular extraversion and anxiety) and also according to the conditions under which the task is set (and more especially if these conditions involve externally imposed stress). Children are therefore divided into two categories, say, with respect to both anxiety (anxious and non-anxious children) and extraversion (extraverted and introverted children) either by the ratings of experienced observers or by the children's scores on suitable questionnaires (such as the Maudsley Personality Inventory for the assessment of introversion–extraversion), and random groups for each of the four cross-classifications are selected. We will suppose that the performance of the task does not depend to any appreciable extent on intelligence, or, alternatively, that the children are sampled from a narrow range of I.Q.s.*

Three levels of conditions are proposed, one being a neutral condition in which the children attempt the task without any induced stress: they

* If the effect of intelligence was considerable, and if the children's I.Q.s ranged widely, intelligence would have to be brought in as an additional factor (in two or more levels), making the experiment one of four factors.

Table 6.1 Scores of twelve groups, in a $2 \times 2 \times 3$ factorial design

		A_1 scores	A_1 cell total	A_2 scores	A_2 cell total
B_2	C_1	29 27 26 24 19	(125)	25 24 23 21 16	(109)
	C_2	27 25 22 21 20	(115)	25 21 20 17 16	(99)
	C_3	26 25 22 19 15	(107)	22 20 20 15 13	(90)
B_1	C_1	26 23 22 21 19	(111)	27 25 24 24 19	(119)
	C_2	24 22 19 19 18	(102)	27 24 23 22 18	(114)
	C_3	22 22 18 17 15	(94)	26 24 21 21 17	(109)

Overall total = 1294

Totals

A_1	654
A_2	640

B_1	649
B_2	645

C_1	464
C_2	430
C_3	400

N.B. The total score of each cell is shown circled.

Key: A_1–Introverted, A_2–Extraverted
B_1–Non-anxious, B_2–Anxious
C_1–Neutral, C_2–Slight stress, C_3–Severe stress

could be told, for instance, that the task was given them merely to find out whether it was suitable for their age group, and that if they did not do well, it would mean merely that the task was not suitable. A second condition would be one in which slight stress would be introduced: thus, the children could be told that they were expected to do well. In a third condition the stress could be made more severe, possibly by telling the children that if they did not do well, it would mean they were not suited to their present class and might be moved elsewhere. Separate, independently selected groups—from each of the anxiety–extraversion cross-classifications—would be tested under these conditions. The experiment would then be a $2 \times 2 \times 3$ factorial experiment, involving twelve independently selected groups in all.

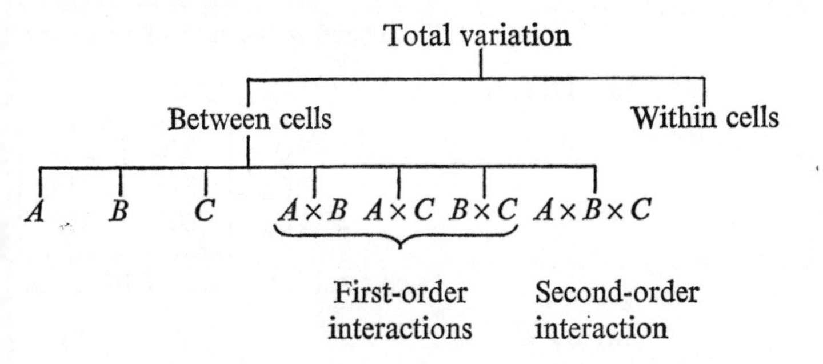

Figure 7 Breakdown of variation in a three-factor experiment

Suppose that five children are selected for each group—in an actual experiment of this nature it would be advisable for the group numbers to be larger, though as before the group numbers would have to be equal or proportionate—and that the test scores are as shown in table 6.1. Each of the sixty scores can be classified in three ways, as belonging to particular levels of extraversion (A), anxiety (B) and conditions of testing (C). Our interest is in the differences between the levels of each of these factors, as well as in the differences arising from the interactions of these factors. There will now be three interactions of the type described in chapter 5—*first-order interactions,* as they are termed—since extraversion interacts with anxiety ($A \times B$), and with conditions ($A \times C$), and anxiety also interacts with conditions ($B \times C$). The sums of squares for all three interactions are a part of the variation between cells (each group of five scores being termed a cell, as before), as also are the sums of squares for differences between the levels of each factor in turn. All these sums, however, do not exhaust the variation between cells. A residual sum is left. This sum measures a *second-order interaction*, that of extraversion, anxiety and conditions ($A \times B \times C$) together (see figure 7).

Table 6.2 Total scores for the cross-classifications of *A*, *B* and *C* taken two at a time (from table 6.1)

(i) $A \times B$

	A_1	A_2
B_2	347	298
B_1	307	342

Each total is the sum of 15 scores.

(ii) $A \times C$

	A_1	A_2
C_1	236	228
C_2	217	213
C_3	201	199

Each total is the sum of 10 scores.

(iii) $B \times C$

	B_1	B_2
C_1	230	234
C_2	216	214
C_3	203	197

Each total is the sum of 10 scores.

Key: A_1–Introverted A_2–Extraverted
B_1–Non-anxious B_2–Anxious
C_1–Neutral C_2–Slight stress C_3–Severe stress

The calculation is as shown below. To facilitate the calculation of the sums of squares for the first-order interactions, table 6.2 has been compiled; this shows the total scores in the cross-classifications of the factors *A*, *B* and *C taken two at a time*. Thus, in section i, showing the $A \times B$ cross-classifications, each cell shows the total of the scores *for all levels of C*.

1. Total sum of squares

$$= \underbrace{(29^2+27^2+\cdots+17^2)}_{\text{Sum of 60 terms}} - \frac{1294\times 1294}{60}$$

$$= 28{,}684 - 27{,}907{\cdot}26$$

$$= 776{\cdot}74$$

2. Between-cells sum of squares

$$= \underbrace{\left(\frac{125^2}{5}+\frac{109^2}{5}+\cdots+\frac{109^2}{5}\right)}_{\text{Sum of 12 terms}} - \frac{1294^2}{60}$$

$$= 28{,}136 - 27{,}907{\cdot}26$$

$$= 228{\cdot}74$$

3. Within-cells sum of squares

$$= 776{\cdot}74 - 228{\cdot}74$$

$$= 548{\cdot}00$$

4. Between A levels sum of squares

$$= \frac{654^2}{30}+\frac{640^2}{30}-\frac{1294^2}{60}$$

$$= 27{,}910{\cdot}53 - 27{,}907{\cdot}26$$

$$= 3{\cdot}27$$

5. Between B levels sum of squares

$$= \frac{645^2}{30}+\frac{659^2}{30}-\frac{1294^2}{60}$$

$$= 27{,}907{\cdot}53 - 27{,}907{\cdot}26$$

$$= 0{\cdot}27$$

6. Between C levels sum of squares

$$= \frac{464^2}{20}+\frac{430^2}{20}+\frac{400^2}{20}-\frac{1294^2}{60}$$

$$= 28{,}009{\cdot}80 - 27{,}907{\cdot}26$$

$$= 102{\cdot}54$$

7. $A\times B$ interaction sum of squares (see table 6.2 i)

$$= \underbrace{\left(\frac{347^2}{15}+\frac{298^2}{15}+\cdots+\frac{342^2}{15}\right)}_{\text{Sum of 4 terms}} - 3{\cdot}27 - 0{\cdot}27 - \frac{1294^2}{60}$$

$$= 28{,}028{\cdot}40 - 3{\cdot}27 - 0{\cdot}27 - 27{,}907{\cdot}26$$

$$= 117{\cdot}60$$

8. $A \times C$ interaction sum of squares (see table 6.2 ii)

$$= \left(\frac{236^2}{10} + \frac{228^2}{10} + \cdots + \frac{199^2}{10}\right) - 3{\cdot}27$$

Sum of 6 terms

$$- 102{\cdot}54 - \frac{1294^2}{60}$$

$$= 28{,}014{\cdot}00 - 3{\cdot}27 - 102{\cdot}54 - 27{,}907{\cdot}26$$

$$= 0{\cdot}93$$

9. $B \times C$ interaction sum of squares (see table 6.2 iii)

$$= \left(\frac{230^2}{10} + \frac{234^2}{10} + \cdots + \frac{197^2}{10}\right) - 0{\cdot}27$$

Sum of 6 terms

$$- 102{\cdot}54 - \frac{1294^2}{60}$$

$$= 28{,}012{\cdot}60 - 0{\cdot}27 - 102{\cdot}54 - 27{,}907{\cdot}26$$

$$= 2{\cdot}53$$

10. $A \times B \times C$ interaction sum of squares

$$= 228{\cdot}74 - 3{\cdot}27 - 0{\cdot}27 - 102{\cdot}54 - 117{\cdot}60 - 0{\cdot}93 - 2{\cdot}53$$

$$= 1{\cdot}60$$

The calculation of the sums of squares for extraversion (A), anxiety (B) and conditions (C)—for the *main effects*, as they are termed—follows the same pattern as before. The sum of squares for each of the first-order interactions is calculated by summing the squares of the cell totals of the appropriate table (table 6.2 i, ii and iii), subtracting the usual correction term and also the sum of squares for each of the two main effects involved. (Thus, for the $A \times B$ interaction the sum of squares for both A and B must be subtracted.) In the same way, when calculating the sum of squares for the second-order interaction—the appropriate cell totals now being those of table 6.1—the sums of squares of all the main effects, A, B and C, and of all the first-order interaction effects, $A \times B$, $A \times C$ and $B \times C$, must be subtracted. The degrees of freedom for the first-order interactions follow the multiplicative rule mentioned earlier (section 5.3); i.e. they are the product of the degrees of freedom for the two relevant main effects. In the same way, the degrees of freedom for the second-order interaction is given by the product of the degrees of freedom for all three main effects.

The sums of squares and degrees of freedom of all effects are set out in table 6.3. The mean squares are also given. Taking the within-cells mean square as the estimate of error,* we see that all effects except two (C and $A \times B$) are clearly insignificant, the F ratios being less than 1. The ratio of the mean square for the $A \times B$ interaction to that for within cells is obtained as

$$F = \frac{117{\cdot}60}{11{\cdot}42} = 10{\cdot}30$$

This for 1 and 48 degrees of freedom is significant at the 1-per-cent level (statistical table 2B).

Table 6.3 Analysis of variance of the data in table 6.1

Source of variation	*Sum of squares*	*Degrees of freedom*	*Mean square*
A	3·27	1	3·27
B	0·27	1	0·27
C	102·54	2	51·27†
$A \times B$	117·60	1	117·60‡
$A \times C$	0·93	2	0·46
$B \times C$	2·53	2	1·26
$A \times B \times C$	1·60	2	0·80
Within cells	548·00	48	11·42
Total	776·74	59	

† Significant at the 5-per-cent level.
‡ Significant at the 1-per-cent level.

To interpret a statistically significant interaction, a table of mean scores for all the cross-classifications is usually prepared. However, with equal numbers in each cross-classification the table of total scores will serve instead. We see from table 6.2 i that the interpretation of the $A \times B$ interaction is strikingly clear. Whereas for anxious children introverts score more highly than extraverts, for non-anxious children it is the extraverts who do better. There is little point in comparing the total (or

* For a fixed-effects model the within-cells mean square provides the estimate of error for all the other effects (see section 6.3).

mean) scores of the introverted and extraverted children—or, again, of the anxious and non-anxious children—as a whole. The introverted children (total score 654) do better than the extraverted (total score 640), though from table 6.3 we see that the difference is not significant. Even if it were significant, however (and a main effect *could* be significant at the same level as a related interaction), the conclusion that introverts do better than extraverts would not have a general validity. It would be limited to children who are anxious.

In precisely the same way, a significant second-order interaction would limit the scope of any first-order interaction involving the same effects. If the $A \times B \times C$ interaction happened to be significant in this investigation, it would mean that the conclusion drawn from the significant $A \times B$ interaction, namely that both the anxious introverts and non-anxious extraverts do better than the other two groups, would not apply to all the levels of C (conditions of testing). If might be found to apply, for instance, only to the neutral and slight stress conditions. As the $A \times B \times C$ interaction is insignificant, however, we may conclude that the superiority of the anxious introverts and non-anxious extraverts applies at all three conditions of testing. An inspection of the totals for $A \times B$ cross-classifications picked out from table 6.1 for the C_1, C_2 and C_3 levels in turn readily confirms this.

The ratio of the mean square for C to that for within cells is

$$F = \frac{51{\cdot}27}{11{\cdot}42} = 4{\cdot}49$$

This, for 2 and 48 degrees of freedom, is significant at the 5-per-cent level (statistical table 2A). From the totals recorded at the bottom of table 6.1, we see that the slight stress condition provides lower scores than the neutral condition, and the severe stress condition lower scores still. Increasing stress has a deleterious influence. Also, since there is no significant interaction involving C, we may conclude that the effect of stress applies equally to anxious and non-anxious, introverted and extraverted children alike.

The significance of the separate differences between the scores at the three levels of C could also be determined in the manner described in section 3.2. The reader is invited to verify that of the three separate differences, only that between the scores at C_1 and C_3, the neutral and severe stress conditions, is significant at the 5-per-cent level.

6.3 The model

With the same notation as that for the model of the two-factor experiment developed in the last chapter (section 5.3), the model may now be set down as

$$x_{ijkl} = M + A_i + B_j + C_k + (AB)_{ij} + (AC)_{ik} + (BC)_{jk} + (ABC)_{ijk} + e_{ijkl}$$

where M is a component common to all the scores;
A_i is a component common to all scores in level i of factor A;
B_j is a component common to all scores in level j of factor B;
C_k is a component common to all scores in level k of factor C;
$(AB)_{ij}$ is a component resulting from the interaction of level i of factor A and level j of factor B;
$(AC)_{ik}$ is a component resulting from the interaction of level i of factor A and level k of factor C;
$(BC)_{jk}$ is a component resulting from the interaction of level j of factor B and level k of factor C;
$(ABC)_{ijk}$ is a component resulting from the interaction of level i of factor A, level j of factor B and level k of factor C;
and e_{ijkl} is a component specific to the score of person l in level i of factor A, level j of factor B and level k of factor C.

Generally i runs from 1 to a, j from 1 to b, and k from 1 to c (in the experiment just described $a = 2$, $b = 2$ and $c = 3$), and with an equal number of scores n in each cell l runs from 1 to n. The nine contributions to the score x_{ijkl} are all independent of each other, and the As, Bs, Cs, (AB)s, (AC)s, (BC)s, (ABC)s and es are regarded as being drawn from normally distributed populations with means of zero and variances of σ_A^2, σ_B^2, σ_C^2, σ_{AB}^2, σ_{AC}^2, σ_{BC}^2, σ_{ABC}^2 and σ^2 respectively (see p. 96).

The components analysis for the case of all three main effects being fixed is shown in table 6.4. The mean-square expectations are a natural extension of those for the two-factor experiment (table 5.5 1). With each of A, B and C fixed, there is no sampling variation from the cross-classifications of A, B and C to influence the cross-classifications taken two at a time—i.e. the first-order interactions—and no sampling variation from any of the cross-classifications to influence the main effects. Notice, too, the balance between subscripts and coefficients: the total number, subscripts plus coefficients, remains the same; and if a particular letter (A say) does not appear as a subscript, the corresponding lower-case letter (*a*) appears as a coefficient. It is apparent from table 6.4 that the within-cells mean square is the appropriate error term for testing the significance of all the other effects.

Table 6.4 Components analysis for a three-factor experiment, all three main effects being fixed

Source of variation	*Degrees of freedom**	*Mean-square expectation*
A	$a-1$	$\sigma^2+nbc\sigma_A^2$
B	$b-1$	$\sigma^2+nac\sigma_B^2$
C	$c-1$	$\sigma^2+nab\sigma_C^2$
$A\times B$	$(a-1)(b-1)$	$\sigma^2+nc\sigma_{AB}^2$
$A\times C$	$(a-1)(c-1)$	$\sigma^2+nb\sigma_{AC}^2$
$B\times C$	$(b-1)(c-1)$	$\sigma^2+na\sigma_{BC}^2$
$A\times B\times C$	$(a-1)(b-1)(c-1)$	$\sigma^2+n\sigma_{ABC}^2$
Within cells	$abc(n-1)$	σ^2

* These are written for a levels of A, b levels of B, c levels of C, and for n scores in each of the abc groups.

We often have to employ a three-way analysis when one of the effects is random. This would be the case if a two-factor experiment—involving methods and levels of intelligence as main effects, for instance—were replicated in a number of schools. Schools would then enter into a three-way analysis as a random effect. Another possibility—though one far less likely to arise in educational investigations—is that two of the three main effects are random. To write out the set of mean-square expectations for each of these cases, it is best to begin with the mean-square expectations when all three main effects are random. These are given in table 6.5. In contrast to table 6.4, we see that the component $n\sigma_{ABC}^2$ enters into all the first-order interactions, and that each of the main effects, too, contains $n\sigma_{ABC}^2$ as well as the components from the two first-order interactions in which it is involved. The balance between subscripts and coefficients remains as before.

Suppose now that one of the effects, C say, is fixed. Certain of the components in the mean-square expectations then have to be deleted.

Schultz (1955) provides a convenient rule for doing this. The rule may be stated as follows:

1. Retain the last component in each line, the component designating the particular effect under consideration.
2. Retain also the first component in each line.
3. Of the remaining components delete those with any subscript representing a fixed effect other than the particular effect under consideration.

Table 6.5 Mean-square expectations for a three-factor experiment, all three main effects being random

Source of variation	*Mean-square expectation**
A	$\sigma^2+n\sigma^2_{ABC}+nc\sigma^2_{AB}+nb\sigma^2_{AC}+nbc\sigma^2_{A}$
B	$\sigma^2+n\sigma^2_{ABC}+nc\sigma^2_{AB}+na\sigma^2_{BC}+nac\sigma^2_{B}$
C	$\sigma^2+n\sigma^2_{ABC}+nb\sigma^2_{AC}+na\sigma^2_{BC}+nab\sigma^2_{C}$
$A\times B$	$\sigma^2+n\sigma^2_{ABC}+nc\sigma^2_{AB}$
$A\times C$	$\sigma^2+n\sigma^2_{ABC}+nb\sigma^2_{AC}$
$B\times C$	$\sigma^2+n\sigma^2_{ABC}+na\sigma^2_{BC}$
$A\times B\times C$	$\sigma^2+n\sigma^2_{ABC}$
Within cells	σ^2

* These are written for *a* levels of *A*, *b* levels of *B*, *c* levels of *C*, and for *n* scores in each of the *abc* groups.

Consider line *A* in table 6.5. The component $n\sigma^2_{ABC}$ contains subscript *C*, which represents a fixed effect and which is not the effect under consideration (*A*); so this component must be deleted. So, too, must the component $nb\sigma^2_{AC}$ in this line. Similarly, in line *B* the components $n\sigma^2_{ABC}$ and $na\sigma^2_{BC}$ must be deleted. In line *C*, on the other hand, the component $n\sigma^2_{ABC}$ has to be retained, since *C* is now the effect under consideration. No component in this line is affected by the rule. The only other component to be deleted is the component $n\sigma^2_{ABC}$ in the line $A\times B$. The resulting mean-square expectations are set out in table 6.6. We see that the $A\times B$ interaction has now to be tested for significance against the within-cells mean square; that the $A\times C$ and $B\times C$ interactions have to be tested against the $A \times B \times C$ mean square; and that the A and B effects have to be tested against the $A \times B$ mean square. No error term for testing the significance of C is provided. An approximate method, based on adding together the C and within-cells mean squares for comparison with the sum of the $A \times C$ and $B \times C$ mean squares, is suggested by Snedecor (1956).

Table 6.6 Mean-square expectations for a three-factor experiment, mixed model, *A* and *B* being random and *C* fixed

Source of variation	*Mean-square expectation**
A	$\sigma^2 + nc\sigma^2_{AB} + nbc\sigma^2_A$
B	$\sigma^2 + nc\sigma^2_{AB} + nac\sigma^2_B$
C	$\sigma^2 + n\sigma^2_{ABC} + nb\sigma^2_{AC} + na\sigma^2_{BC} + nab\sigma^2_C$
$A \times B$	$\sigma^2 + nc\sigma^2_{AB}$
$A \times C$	$\sigma^2 + n\sigma^2_{ABC} + nb\sigma^2_{AC}$
$B \times C$	$\sigma^2 + n\sigma^2_{ABC} + na\sigma^2_{BC}$
$A \times B \times C$	$\sigma^2 + n\sigma^2_{ABC}$
Within cells	σ^2

* These are written for a levels of A, b levels of B, c levels of C, and for n scores in each of the abc groups.

If, in addition to C, B is also fixed, further deletions must be made. In line A of table 6.6, for instance, the component $nc\sigma^2_{AB}$ contains subscript B and so has to be deleted. The reader will have no difficulty in showing that the mean-square expectations will then be as given in table 6.7. We see that the A and $A \times C$ effects, as well as those of $A \times B$ and $A \times B \times C$, have now to be tested for significance against the within-cells mean square; that the $B \times C$ interaction still has to be tested against the $A \times B \times C$ mean square; that the B effect is still tested against the $A \times B$ mean square; and that C can now be tested against the $A \times C$ mean square. If, finally, the A effect is also fixed, further application of Schultz's rule would yield the mean-square expectations already shown in table 6.4.

Table 6.7 Mean-square expectations for a three-factor experiment, mixed model, A being random and B and C fixed

Source of variation	*Mean-square expectation**
A	$\sigma^2+nbc\sigma_A^2$
B	$\sigma^2+nc\sigma_{AB}^2+nac\sigma_B^2$
C	$\sigma^2+nb\sigma_{AC}^2+nab\sigma_C^2$
$A\times B$	$\sigma^2+nc\sigma_{AB}^2$
$A\times C$	$\sigma^2+nb\sigma_{AC}^2$
$B\times C$	$\sigma^2+n\sigma_{ABC}^2+na\sigma_{BC}^2$
$A\times B\times C$	$\sigma^2+n\sigma_{ABC}^2$
Within cells	σ^2

* These are written for a levels of A, b levels of B, c levels of C, and for n scores in each of the abc groups.

6.4 Orthogonal comparisons

Each of the sources of variation separated out in table 6.3 may be derived from an orthogonal comparison of the various cross-classifications. The variation represented in the first seven lines of the table—accounting for 11 degrees of freedom—may, in fact, be derived from eleven independent orthogonal comparisons. The total scores in each of the cross-classifications of A, B and C (taken from table 6.1) are set out again in table 6.8, at the head of the columns giving the λ coefficients for the comparisons (see section 3.5). We note that the sum of the coefficients in any one row is zero, as is also the sum of the products of corresponding coefficients in any two rows. Multiplying each coefficient by the score at the head of the column and then adding for each row gives the comparison sums (c) shown on the right. For the rows A and B these c sums could have been obtained from the main-effects totals in table 6.1, i.e. $A_1-A_2 = 14$ and $B_1-B_2 = 4$. Two rows have been written for the main effect C. This is because C has 2 degrees of freedom, and these have been resolved (arbitrarily) into (a) 1 degree of freedom for the difference between the level C_1 and the average of the levels C_2 and C_3, and (b) 1 degree of freedom for the difference between C_2 and C_3.

Table 6.8 Orthogonal comparisons for the 2×2×3 experiment (table 6.1)

Total cross-classification scores

Comparison		$A_1B_1C_1$ 111	$A_1B_1C_2$ 102	$A_1B_1C_3$ 94	$A_1B_2C_1$ 125	$A_1B_2C_2$ 115	$A_1B_2C_3$ 107	$A_2B_1C_1$ 119
A		−1	−1	−1	−1	−1	−1	1
B		−1	−1	−1	1	1	1	−1
C	(i)	2	−1	−1	2	−1	−1	2
	(ii)	0	1	−1	0	1	−1	0
$A \times B$		1	1	1	−1	−1	−1	−1
$A \times C$	(i)	−2	1	1	−2	1	1	2
	(ii)	0	−1	1	0	−1	1	0
$B \times C$	(i)	−2	1	1	2	−1	−1	−2
	(ii)	0	−1	1	0	1	−1	0
$A \times B \times C$	(i)	2	−1	−1	−2	1	1	−2
	(ii)	0	1	−1	0	−1	1	0

	A_1	A_2
B_2	347	298
B_1	307	342

The coefficients for the interactions have been obtained by multiplication. For the $A \times B$ comparison, for instance, corresponding coefficients in the A and B rows have been multiplied, and for each of the $A \times B \times C$ comparisons corresponding coefficients in the A, B and the particular C row have been multiplied. The comparison sum for $A \times B$ could have been obtained from table 6.2 i, reproduced above for convenience.

Table 6.8 (continued)

Total cross-classification scores							*Sum of squares*
$A_2B_1C_2$ 114	$A_2B_1C_3$ 109	$A_2B_2C_1$ 109	$A_2B_2C_2$ 99	$A_2B_2C_3$ 90	*Sum* (*c*)	$\Sigma\lambda^2$	$\left(\frac{c^2}{n\,\Sigma\lambda^2}\right)$
1	1	1	1	1	14	12	3·27
−1	−1	1	1	1	−4	12	0·27
−1	−1	2	−1	−1	98	24	80·03 } 102·53
1	−1	0	1	−1	30	8	22·50
−1	−1	1	1	1	−84	12	117·60
−1	−1	2	−1	−1	−10	24	0·83 } 0·93
1	−1	0	1	−1	−2	8	0·10
1	1	2	−1	−1	16	24	2·13 } 2·53
−1	1	0	1	−1	4	8	0·40
1	1	2	−1	−1	12	24	1·20 } 1·60
−1	1	0	1	−1	4	8	0·40

The difference $B_2 - B_1$ at level A_2 is $298-342 = -44$, and the same difference at level A_1 is $347-307 = 40$; so the change in the difference is $-44-40 = -84$, as given in table 6.8.

The sum of squares for each comparison is evaluated by the formula $\frac{c^2}{n\,\Sigma\,\lambda^2}$, $\Sigma\,\lambda^2$ being the sum of the squares of the coefficients, and n the number of scores in each group, 5. The sums for the two separate comparisons of C, $A \times C$ and $A \times B \times C$ have been combined. All the sums of squares are seen to agree exactly with those previously obtained (table 6.3), except for a small discrepancy in one instance (0·01) due to rounding error.

The orthogonal comparisons for the case of A, B and C all having two

Table 6.9 Orthogonal comparisons for a 2×2×2 experiment

Comparison	*Total cross-classification scores*								*Sum* (*c*)
	$A_1B_1C_1$ $a_1b_1c_1$	$A_1B_1C_2$ $a_1b_1c_2$	$A_1B_2C_1$ $a_1b_2c_1$	$A_1B_2B_2$ $a_1b_2c_2$	$A_2B_1C_1$ $a_2b_1c_1$	$A_2B_1C_2$ $a_2b_1c_2$	$A_2B_2C_1$ $a_2b_2c_1$	$A_2B_2C_2$ $a_2b_2c_2$	
A	−1	−1	−1	−1	1	1	1	1	c_A
B	−1	−1	1	1	−1	−1	1	1	c_B
C	−1	1	−1	1	−1	1	−1	1	c_C
$A \times B$	1	1	−1	−1	−1	−1	1	1	$c_{A \times B}$
$A \times C$	1	−1	1	−1	−1	1	−1	1	$c_{A \times C}$
$B \times C$	1	−1	−1	1	1	−1	−1	1	$c_{B \times C}$
$A \times B \times C$	−1	1	1	−1	1	−1	−1	1	$c_{A \times B \times C}$

levels is of special interest, in that each comparison then represents one of the between-cells sources of variance in the analysis of variance. The comparisons are set out in table 6.9. If the total scores for the various cross-classifications are shown by the appropriate lower-case letters, then the comparison sum for A appears as

$$c_A = -a_1b_1c_1 - a_1b_1c_2 - a_1b_2c_1 - a_1b_2c_2 + a_2b_1c_1 + a_2b_1c_2 + a_2b_2c_1 + a_2b_2c_2$$

This we can represent formally as

$$c_A = (a_2 - a_1)(b_2 + b_1)(c_2 + c_1)$$

since if this expression were expanded algebraically, the former expression would be obtained.

In the same way, the comparison sums for B and C may be represented as

$$c_B = (a_2 + a_1)(b_2 - b_1)(c_2 + c_1)$$

and

$$c_C = (a_2 + a_1)(b_2 + b_1)(c_2 - c_1)$$

The comparison sums for the interactions may also be represented in this manner. The $A \times B$ sum, for instance, is

$$c_{A \times B} = a_1b_1c_1 + a_1b_1c_2 - a_1b_2c_1 - a_1b_2c_2 - a_2b_1c_1 - a_2b_1c_2 + a_2b_2c_1 + a_2b_2c_2$$

which may be represented by

$$c_{A \times B} = (a_2 - a_1)(b_2 - b_1)(c_2 + c_1)$$

Similarly we may write

$$c_{A \times C} = (a_2 - a_1)(b_2 + b_1)(c_2 - c_1)$$

and

$$c_{B \times C} = (a_2 + a_1)(b_2 - b_1)(c_2 - c_1)$$

Finally, the comparison sum for the second-order interaction, which is given by

$$c_{A \times B \times C} = -a_1b_1c_1 + a_1b_1c_2 + a_1b_2c_1 - a_1b_2c_2 + a_2b_1c_1 - a_2b_1c_2 - a_2b_2c_1 + a_2b_2c_2$$

may be represented by

$$c_{A \times B \times C} = (a_2 - a_1)(b_2 - b_1)(c_2 - c_1)$$

Similar expressions may be written for main and interaction effects of experiments with more than three factors. Discussion of this now follows.

A further simplification adopted by many writers is to represent the *upper* level of the factor by the lower-case letter and the lower level by the absence of the letter. Thus, the cross-classification sum for $A_2B_2C_2$ would be written as *abc*, the sum for $A_1B_2C_2$ as *bc*, the sum for $A_1B_1C_2$ as *c* and the sum for $A_1B_1C_1$ simply as (1). The comparison sum, $A \times B \times C$, for instance, would then appear as $(-1)+c+b-bc+a-ac-ab+abc$, which may be represented by $(a-1)(b-1)(c-1)$.

6.5 Higher dimensional designs

When the number of factors exceeds three, the number and variety of the different effects increases rapidly. With four factors (A, B, C and D) we would have in addition to the four main effects six first-order interactions ($A \times B$, $A \times C$, $A \times D$, $B \times C$, $B \times D$ and $C \times D$), four second-order interactions ($A \times B \times C$, $A \times B \times D$, $A \times C \times D$ and $B \times C \times D$) and one third-order interaction ($A \times B \times C \times D$). Similarly, with five factors we would have five main effects, ten first-order interactions, ten second-order interactions, five third-order interactions and one fourth-order interaction. The degrees of freedom for these effects follow the same pattern as before.

Each higher-order interaction, if statistically significant, will limit the scope of any conclusion drawn from a lower-order interaction (involving the same factors), just as a significant first-order interaction will limit the scope of a related main effect. Higher-order interactions may be interpreted in a number of ways. The third-order $A \times B \times C \times D$ interaction, for instance, may be regarded as the interaction of $A \times B \times C$ with D, i.e. as differences in the interaction $A \times B \times C$ at the various levels of D, or as the interaction of $A \times B \times D$ with C, or as the interaction of $A \times C \times D$ with B, or as the interaction of $B \times C \times D$ with A. It may also be regarded as the interaction between the two first-order interactions $A \times B$ and $C \times D$—or again, between $A \times C$ and $B \times D$, etc.—i.e. as differences in the $A \times B$ interactions as different levels of both C and D are taken in turn.

An orderly arrangement of the data can be made without difficulty, though the actual computations become increasingly laborious. Take, for example, a third-order interaction ($A \times B \times C \times D$) in a five-factor design. The sum of squares of the cell totals from the appropriate table is obtained —the table giving the cross-classifications of the four factors A, B, C and D, the total score in each cell being the sum for all levels of E—and from this sum is subtracted the sum of squares for each of the four main effects involved (A, B, C and D), the sum of squares for each of the six first-order interactions involved ($A \times B$, $A \times C$, $A \times D$, $B \times C$, $B \times D$ and $C \times D$), and the sum of squares for each of the four second-order interactions involved ($A \times B \times C$, $A \times B \times D$, $A \times C \times D$ and $B \times C \times D$), and finally the correction term.*

Because of the arithmetical labour of a complete analysis, a frequent practice has been to calculate sums of squares for the main effects and first- and second-order interactions only, taking the mean square from the residual sum of squares as the error term. This practice assumes that all the higher-order interactions are insignificant, or, more precisely, that all the population variances of type σ^2_{ABC}, σ^2_{ABCD}, etc., are zero. If this happens to be true, and if the model has only fixed effects, then the mean square from each of the unseparated interactions estimates the same population variance, σ^2. By taking the mean square from the residual sum—a composite of all these interaction sums and the within-cells sum—one is in effect pooling all the separate sums to get a better estimate, i.e. one based on a larger number of degrees of freedom. If, on the other hand, one or more of the population variances σ^2_{ABC}, σ^2_{ABCD}, etc., is not zero, the residual mean square can be expected to over-estimate σ^2 (for a fixed-effects model) and significance tests based on it will fail too frequently to detect real differences. Unless, therefore, there is reason to believe (from previous experiments) that all third- and higher-order interactions are in fact negligible, this practice is not recommended.

For a model with one or more random effects, the choice of error term for any particular effect must be worked out systematically by writing down the full components analysis—i.e. an analysis for a model with only random effects—and then deleting appropriate components in accordance with Schultz's rule. Interactions between the random and fixed effects are generally to be expected, and the use of a residual mean square derived from an incomplete analysis should again be discouraged.

Complete factorial designs with four or more factors are, in fact, seldom employed in educational research. This is because with a large number of factors, and also with a large number of levels for each factor, the experiment becomes unwieldy. Even if we tested only five factors, each with only two levels, we would have 2^5 or thirty-two cross-classifications in all, i.e. thirty-two separate groups for testing. The administrative and other practical difficulties involved might then be prohibitive.

* For variants of this method of calculation, which may occasionally be useful, see Edwards and Horst (1950).

An obvious advantage would be to have all levels of some of the factors administered to the same group of testees, if this is possible. (For many factors it is not: different methods of teaching, for instance, inevitably necessitate different groups.) Designs which allow all levels of *some* of the factors to be administered to the same testees are described in chapter 7. When the same group cannot be used for more than one level of a factor, an 'incomplete' factorial design may sometimes be helpful. This is a design in which some of the information possible from the complete factorial design is sacrificed. Usually the information sacrificed will be a higher-order interaction expected, from previous experiment in the field, to be negligible (factorial experiments with confounding), though it could also involve a main effect (the split-plot design). Detailed accounts are provided by Cochran and Cox (1957).*

* The basic principle is the use of blocks, similar to that of a randomized-blocks design (figure 4), each block containing only some of the possible cross-classifications, but with the differences between blocks being eliminated from statistical error as before. Thus, suppose that two such blocks for a $2 \times 2 \times 2$ experiment are (in the notation suggested at the end of section 6.4) as follows:

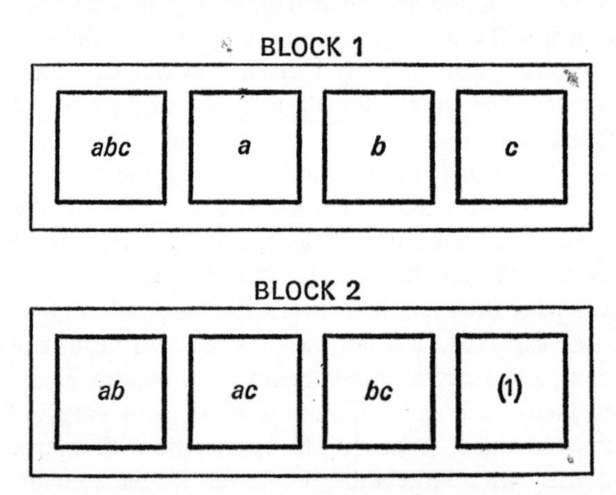

Two of the plots in each block contain the upper level of A, and two the lower level of A. Hence the A effect is unaffected by the differences between the block. Similarly, we can verify (from table 6.9) that each of the B, C, $A \times B$, $A \times C$ and $B \times C$ effects is also unaffected by the difference between the blocks. The $A \times B \times C$ effect, however, is based on the comparison $abc+a+b+c-ab-ac-bc-(1)$, i.e. block 1 plots minus block 2 plots. The second-order interaction is *confounded* (inseparable in its effect) with the difference between the blocks.

References

COCHRAN, W. G. and COX, G. M. (1957) *Experimental Designs*, New York: Wiley (2nd edition), pp. 183–212 and 293–305.

EDWARDS, A. L. and HORST, P. (1950) 'The calculation of sums of squares for interactions in the analysis of variance,' *Psychometrika*, **15**, 17–24.

FISHER, R. A. (1951) *The Design of Experiments*, Edinburgh: Oliver & Boyd (6th edition), pp. 91–100.

SCHULTZ, E. F. (1955) 'Rules of thumb for determining expectations of mean squares,' *Biometrics*, **11**, 123–35.

SNEDECOR, G. W. (1956) *Statistical Methods*, Iowa State College Press (5th edition), pp. 359–63.

Chapter 7 Designs with Nesting and Crossing

7.1 A single crossing of the nested factor

To illustrate a basic design involving both nesting and crossing, a study in the field of programmed learning (Lewis and Gregson 1965) may be taken. The study is concerned with the effect of frame size on learning from a linear programme. It is generally accepted that a sequence of fairly small steps is necessary for the mastery of complex material, yet differing views may be held as to how much material can best be presented at the same time. The same basic programme—one dealing with the history of number—was therefore presented in three versions according to the size of frame, large, medium and small. Pupils drawn from three ability groups (relatively high, medium and low I.Q.s) were selected, equal numbers from each group being allocated at random to each programme frame size. After the programme was worked through, an immediate test was given. The same test was given again just over a week later, and also on a third occasion a month later. Scores were therefore obtained from three I.Q. groups, with respect to three frame sizes on three occasions. The scores are set out in table 7.1.

We see that the experiment resembles a $3 \times 3 \times 3$ factorial experiment, frame size, I.Q. and occasions being the three factors. One essential difference, however, should be noted between a comparison of the different levels of frame size and I.Q. on the one hand, and of the different levels of occasions on the other. Different levels of frame size and I.Q. contain the scores of *different* pupils, while all the occasions contain the scores of the *same* pupils. Pupils, in other words, appears as an additional factor, one which is nested within frame size and I.Q. but which, within each of the cross-classifications of frame size and I.Q., is crossed with occasions. The experiment has therefore been described as a four-way experiment in table 7.1, since each score may be classified in four ways, i.e. as belonging to a particular frame size (A), I.Q. group (B), occasion (C), and pupil.

		A_1							A_2							A_3						
B_3	C_1	117	96	111	104	110	108	(646)	113	102	97	114	110	111	(647)	117	94	101	118	113	82	(625)
	C_2	103	90	83	85	97	85	(543)	92	101	89	75	106	93	(556)	104	80	97	117	113	72	(583)
	C_3	114	88	78	83	113	79	(555)	106	105	91	80	98	46	(526)	98	69	100	114	109	75	(565)
	Total	334	274	272	272	320	272	[1744]	311	308	277	269	314	250	[1729]	319	243	298	349	335	229	[1773]
B_2	C_1	107	108	113	114	116	85	(643)	98	111	90	104	87	98	(588)	108	106	70	64	94	101	(543)
	C_2	68	89	82	103	97	48	(487)	102	93	72	96	46	68	(477)	95	77	57	64	76	85	(454)
	C_3	65	68	88	71	90	59	(441)	93	91	67	96	34	67	(448)	95	76	61	60	66	73	(431)
	Total	240	265	283	288	303	192	[1571]	293	295	229	296	167	233	[1513]	298	259	188	188	236	259	[1428]
B_1	C_1	102	51	96	111	91	109	(560)	96	100	53	87	62	95	(493)	103	83	78	102	53	77	(496)
	C_2	92	34	69	69	76	84	(424)	72	77	48	86	52	69	(404)	77	74	72	79	34	42	(378)
	C_3	76	46	60	73	74	67	(396)	89	89	56	85	57	61	(437)	84	81	73	104	40	61	(443)
	Total	270	131	225	253	241	260	[1380]	257	266	157	258	171	225	[1334]	264	238	223	285	127	180	[1317]

Totals

A_1	4695	B_1	4031	C_1	5241
A_2	4576	B_2	4512	C_2	4306
A_3	4518	B_3	5246	C_3	4242

Overall total = 13,789

N.B. The totals for each of the twenty-seven ABC cross-classifications are shown circled.
Within each of the nine AB cross-classifications the scores in the same column belong to the same pupil.
The totals for each of the nine AB cross-classifications are shown boxed.

Key: A_1–Small frame size; A_2–Medium frame size; A_3–Large frame size
B_1–Low I.Q.s; B_2–Average I.Q.s; B_3–High I.Q.s
C_1–Occasion 1; C_2–Occasion 2; C_3–Occasion 3

The analysis of the differences between cells—a cell being one of the *ABC* cross-classifications, as before—follows the same pattern as in section 6.2, the sums of squares for the main effects of frame size, I.Q. and occasions being separated as well as those for the three first-order and one second-order interaction between these effects. In addition, however, a sum of squares for the differences between pupils must now be removed from the variation within the $A \times B$ cross-classifications,* leaving a residual sum representing the interaction of pupils with occasions, again within the $A \times B$ cross-classifications. The calculation is shown below. The first ten steps parallel those of the analysis in section 6.2.

1. Total sum of squares

$$= \underbrace{(117^2+96^2+\cdots+61^2)}_{\text{Sum of 162 terms}} - \frac{13{,}789\times 13{,}789}{162}$$
$$= 1{,}239{,}847 - 1{,}173{,}682{\cdot}23$$
$$= 66{,}164{\cdot}77$$

2. Between-cells sum of squares

$$= \underbrace{\left(\frac{646^2}{6}+\frac{647^2}{6}+\cdots+\frac{443^2}{6}\right)}_{\text{Sum of 27 terms}} - \frac{13{,}789^2}{162}$$
$$= 1{,}202{,}121{\cdot}17 - 1{,}173{,}682{\cdot}23$$
$$= 28{,}438{\cdot}94$$

3. Within-cells sum of squares

$$= 66{,}164{\cdot}77 - 28{,}438{\cdot}94$$
$$= 37{,}725{\cdot}83$$

4. Between *A* levels sum of squares

$$= \frac{4695^2}{54}+\frac{4576^2}{54}+\frac{4518^2}{54}-\frac{13{,}789^2}{162}$$
$$= 1{,}173{,}983{\cdot}80 - 1{,}173{,}682{\cdot}23$$
$$= 301{\cdot}57$$

5. Between *B* levels sum of squares

$$= \frac{4031^2}{54}+\frac{4512^2}{54}+\frac{5246^2}{54}-\frac{13{,}789^2}{162}$$
$$= 1{,}187{,}548{\cdot}54 - 1{,}173{,}682{\cdot}23$$
$$= 13{,}866{\cdot}31$$

* This was not possible in the experiment of section 6.2, since there each cell contained the scores of independent groups, i.e. of *different* children.

6. Between C levels sum of squares
$$= \frac{5241^2}{54} + \frac{4306^2}{54} + \frac{4242^2}{54} - \frac{13{,}789^2}{162}$$
$$= 1{,}185{,}264{\cdot}46 - 1{,}173{,}682{\cdot}23$$
$$= 11{,}582{\cdot}23$$

7. $A \times B$ interaction sum of squares
$$= \underbrace{\left(\frac{1744^2}{18} + \frac{1729^2}{18} + \cdots + \frac{1317^2}{18}\right)}_{\text{Sum of 9 terms}} - 301{\cdot}57 - 13{,}866{\cdot}31 - \frac{13{,}789^2}{162}$$
$$= 1{,}188{,}296{\cdot}94 - 301{\cdot}57 - 13{,}866{\cdot}31 - 1{,}173{,}682{\cdot}23$$
$$= 446{\cdot}83$$

8. $A \times C$ interaction sum of squares (see table 7.2 i)
$$= \underbrace{\left(\frac{1849^2}{18} + \frac{1728^2}{18} + \cdots + \frac{1439^2}{18}\right)}_{\text{Sum of 9 terms}} - 301{\cdot}57 - 11{,}582{\cdot}23 - \frac{13{,}789^2}{162}$$
$$= 1{,}186{,}349{\cdot}83 - 301{\cdot}57 - 11{,}582{\cdot}23 - 1{,}173{,}682{\cdot}23$$
$$= 783{\cdot}80$$

9. $B \times C$ interaction sum of squares (see table 7.2 ii)
$$= \underbrace{\left(\frac{1918^2}{18} + \frac{1682^2}{18} + \cdots + \frac{1646^2}{18}\right)}_{\text{Sum of 9 terms}} - 13{,}866{\cdot}31 - 11{,}582{\cdot}23 - \frac{13{,}789^2}{162}$$
$$= 1{,}199{,}965{\cdot}39 - 13{,}866{\cdot}31 - 11{,}582{\cdot}23 - 1{,}173{,}682{\cdot}23$$
$$= 834{\cdot}62$$

10. $A \times B \times C$ interaction sum of squares
$$= 28{,}438{\cdot}94 - 301{\cdot}57 - 13{,}866{\cdot}31 - 11{,}582{\cdot}23 - 446{\cdot}83 - 783{\cdot}80 - 834{\cdot}62$$
$$= 623{\cdot}58$$

Table 7.2 Total scores for the $A \times C$ and $B \times C$ cross-classifications in table 7.1

(i) $A \times C$

	A_1	A_2	A_3
C_1	1849	1728	1664
C_2	1454	1437	1415
C_3	1392	1411	1439

(ii) $B \times C$

	C_1	C_2	C_3
B_3	1918	1682	1646
B_2	1774	1418	1320
B_1	1549	1206	1276

N.B. Totals for the $A \times B$ cross-classifications are recorded in table 7.1.

Key: A_1–Small frame size, A_2–Medium frame size, A_3–Large frame size
B_1–Low I.Q.s, B_2–Average I.Q.s, B_3–High I.Q.s
C_1–Occasion 1, C_2–Occasion 2, C_3–Occasion 3

---

11. Between-pupils (P) (within $A \times B$) sum of squares

$$= \left(\frac{334^2}{3} + \frac{274^2}{3} + \cdots + \frac{272^2}{3}\right) - \frac{1744^2}{18}*$$

Sum of 6 terms

$$+ \left(\frac{311^2}{3} + \frac{308^2}{3} + \cdots + \frac{250^2}{3}\right) - \frac{1729^2}{18}$$

Sum of 6 terms

+ Similar sets of terms for each of the other seven $A \times B$ cross-classifications

$$= 30{,}672{\cdot}20$$

12. Residual sum of squares ($P \times C$ interaction, within $A \times B$)

$$= 37{,}725{\cdot}83 - 30{,}672{\cdot}20$$
$$= 7{,}053{\cdot}63$$

* Each of the numerators 334, 274, ··· 272 is the sum of three scores; 1744 is the sum of eighteen scores.

The first ten steps in the calculation are similar to those described for the factorial experiment in chapter 6.* For the between-pupils sum of squares, separate correction terms are subtracted for each of the $A \times B$ cross-classifications. This sum is a measure of the pupil differences within each of the $A \times B$ cross-classifications, and totalled for all of those cross-classifications. As there are six pupils and therefore 5 degrees of freedom within each cross-classification, the degrees of freedom for this sum are 45.

Table 7.3 Analysis of variance of the data in table 7.1

Source of variation	*Sum of squares*	*Degrees of freedom*	*Mean square*
A	301·57	2	150·78
B	13,866·31	2	6,933·15†
C	11,582·23	2	5,791·11†
$A \times B$	446·83	4	111·71
$A \times C$	783·80	4	195·95‡
$B \times C$	834·62	4	208·65‡
$A \times B \times C$	623·58	8	77·95
Pupils (P), within $A \times B$	30,672·20	45	681·60
Residual ($P \times C$), within $A \times B$	7,053·63	90	78·37
Total	66,164·77	161	

† Significant at the 5-per-cent level.
‡ Significant at the 1-per-cent level.

In the same way, the residual sum of squares is a measure of the variation remaining within the $A \times B$ cross-classifications after the removal of the pupil differences. As the only main effects are those of occasions and pupils, and as both have already been removed, this residual sum may

* The partitioning of the total sum of squares for the present experiment has been described in this way, as it is an extension of that described in chapter 6. An alternative approach would be that of separating the total sum of squares into sums for between pupils and within pupils, A, B and $A \times B$ being subdivisions of the former sum and C, $A \times C$, $B \times C$ and $A \times B \times C$ subdivisions of the latter (see Lindquist 1956).

therefore be described as the sum for the pupils × occasions interaction within each of the frame size × I.Q. cross-classifications, and totalled for all such cross-classifications. The sum has been obtained by subtracting the between-pupils sum (306,672·00) from the within-cells sum (37,725·83). The degrees of freedom may also be obtained in this way, i.e. $135-45 = 90$. (Alternatively, as there are six pupils (P) and three occasions (C), and therefore $5\times 2 = 10$ degrees of freedom, for the $P\times C$ interaction within each of the nine $A\times B$ cross-classifications, the degrees of freedom may be obtained as $10\times 9 = 90$.)

The analysis of variance is set out in table 7.3. There are two error terms, the mean square for pupils (P), and that for the residual ($P\times C$ within $A\times B$). The mean square for pupils is the error term for all effects based on sets of scores from different pupils, i.e. frame size (A), I.Q. (B) and the $A\times B$ interaction. The residual mean square is the error term for all other effects, i.e. those involving occasions (C), and therefore based on sets of scores from the same pupils. The justification for this is postponed until the next section.

Taking first the effects testable by the mean square for pupils, we have the following F ratios:

for A, $F = \dfrac{150{\cdot}78}{681{\cdot}60} < 1$, so that the differences in frame size are not statistically significant;

for B, $F = \dfrac{6{,}933{\cdot}15}{681{\cdot}60} = 10{\cdot}17$, which for 2 and 45 degrees of freedom is significant at the 1-per-cent level (statistical table 2B);

and for $A\times B$, $F = \dfrac{111{\cdot}71}{681{\cdot}60} < 1$, so that the frame size × intelligence interaction is not statistically significant.

For the effects testable by the residual mean square we have

for C, $F = \dfrac{5{,}791{\cdot}11}{78{\cdot}37} = 73{\cdot}87$, which for 2 and 90 degrees of freedom is significant at the 1-per-cent level (statistical table 2B);

for $A \times C$, $F = \dfrac{195{\cdot}95}{78{\cdot}37} = 2{\cdot}50$, which for 4 and 90 degrees of freedom is significant at the 5-per-cent level (statistical table 2A);

for $B \times C$, $F = \dfrac{208{\cdot}65}{78{\cdot}37} = 2{\cdot}66$, which for 4 and 90 degrees of freedom is significant at the 5-per-cent level (statistical table 2A);

and for $A \times B \times C$, $F = \dfrac{77{\cdot}95}{78{\cdot}37} < 1$, so that the frame size × intelligence × occasions interaction is not statistically significant.

The total scores for the $A \times C$ and $B \times C$ cross-classifications (upon which the two significant interactions are based) have been set out in table 7.2. In the $A \times C$ table we see that, while on the first occasion the scores decrease sharply with increasing frame size, on the second this decrease is only slight, and on the third the trend is actually reversed (though only to a slight extent). Learning from the large frames appears at an advantage only on the most delayed test. Clearly it is this difference in trend which underlies the significance of the frame size × conditions interaction. Again, since the second-order interaction ($A \times B \times C$) is not significant, this difference in trend may be held to be the same at all three levels of I.Q.

An inspection of the $B \times C$ table shows that although the scores at both the high and average I.Q. levels decrease as we proceed from occasion 1 to 3, the score at the low I.Q. level increases (slightly) on occasion 3, though remaining well below that for occasion 1. Alternatively, viewing the column trends, we may say that the decrease in score when proceeding to the lowest I.Q.s is less pronounced on occasion 3. Again, from the insignificant second-order interaction, this feature may be taken as fundamentally the same for all three frame sizes. For both the $A \times C$ and $B \times C$ tables the significance of the difference between any two scores in the same row or column could well be tested in the manner previously described (section 3.2).

The differential influence of occasions on the differences between I.Q. levels is the only qualification we need to make in interpreting the significance of the main effect of I.Q. Overall the high I.Q. group does markedly better than the average I.Q. group, and the average I.Q. group markedly better than the low I.Q. group. (See the total scores recorded at the bottom of table 7.1.)

The main effect of frame size, on the other hand, is far too small for statistical significance, though we see from the total scores that learning from the small frames appears more effective than from the medium frames, and learning from the medium frames more effective than from the large frames. As has been noted, the superiority of the small frames is most marked for occasion 1. Indeed, it is the differential effect of occasions on frame size which has been shown to be important. Similarly the expected and significant decrease in score on the later occasions needs to be qualified by the two significant interactions described.

7.2 The model for a single crossing of the nested factor

The model for the design of the programmed learning experiment described may be written as

$$x_{ijkl} = M + A_i + B_j + C_k + (AB)_{ij} + (AC)_{ik} + (BC)_{jk} + (ABC)_{ijk} + P_{ijl} + (PC)_{ijkl}$$

The first eight terms are identical with those of the model for the three-factor experiment of chapter 6 (section 6.3), with A now referring to frame size, B to intelligence and C to occasion. P_{ijl} is a component common to all the scores of pupil l of level i of factor A and level j of factor B, while the term $(PC)_{ijkl}$—which could also be written more simply, though less descriptively, as e_{ijkl}—is a component specific to the score of pupil l (again of level i of factor A and level j of factor B) on occasion k. Note that the subscript l occurs only with the accompanying subscripts i and j, so expressing the nesting of pupils within frame size and intelligence. In the particular experiment described, i, j and k all run from 1 to 3, while l runs from 1 to 6.

The components analysis is shown in table 7.4. The balance between subscripts and coefficients in the components of the mean-square expectations is maintained by using a dot to precede the factors within which the factor pupils (P) is nested. $\sigma^2_{P.AB}$, therefore, denotes the variance of pupils within the frame size and intelligence cross-classifications, and $\sigma^2_{PC.AB}$ the variance of the interaction between pupils and occasions again within the frame size and intelligence cross-classifications. With this notation, we see that the number of subscripts and coefficients is the same for all components, and that if a particular factor does not appear as a subscript, the corresponding lower-case letter appears as a coefficient.

Table 7.4 Components analysis for a four-factor experiment, one factor being nested and singly crossed

Source of variation	*Degrees of freedom**	*Mean-square expectation*†
A	$a-1$	$\sigma^2_{PA.BC}+c\sigma^2_{P.AB}+pbc\sigma^2_A$
B	$b-1$	$\sigma^2_{PC.AB}+c\sigma^2_{P.AB}+pac\sigma^2_B$
C	$c-1$	$\sigma^2_{PC.AB}+pab\sigma^2_C$
$A\times B$	$(a-1)(b-1)$	$\sigma^2_{PC.AB}+c\sigma^2_{P.AB}+pc\sigma^2_{AB}$
$A\times C$	$(a-1)(c-1)$	$\sigma^2_{PC.AB}+pb\sigma^2_{AC}$
$B\times C$	$(b-1)(c-1)$	$\sigma^2_{PC.AB}+pa\sigma^2_{BC}$
$A\times B\times C$	$(a-1)(b-1)(c-1)$	$\sigma^2_{PC.AB}+p\sigma^2_{ABC}$
P, within $A\times B$	$ab(p-1)$	$\sigma^2_{PC.AB}+c\sigma^2_{P.AB}$
$P\times C$, within $A\times B$	$ab(p-1)(c-1)$	$\sigma^2_{PC.AB}$

* These are written for a levels of A, b levels of B, c levels of C and p levels of P within each of the ab cross-classifications of A and B.

† A, B and C are taken to be fixed effects, and P a random effect.

It is best to begin setting out the mean-square expectations from the bottom upwards (i.e. starting with the basic variation $P\times C$, within $A\times B$) on the assumption that all effects are random, deletions for fixedness afterwards being made in accordance with Schultz's rule. One further point, however, needs to be made respecting these deletions. A component can qualify for deletion in the case of nesting only in respect of subscripts *preceding* the dot. (The subscripts are referred to by Schultz (1955) as 'essential'.) A component is not deleted because of the fixedness of any effect specified by a subscript after the dot. The components for the case of all effects being random are shown at the top of p. 142, the subsequent deletions for the fixedness of A, B and C being indicated by oblique lines.

With the deletions indicated, these mean-square expectations become identical with those in table 7.4. It follows that the residual mean square (from $P\times C$, within $A\times B$) is the correct error term for testing the

Table 7.5 Scores of two groups in a four-way experiment

		A_1	A_2	*Total* (A_1+A_2)
C_1	B_1	5 8 7 2 7 7 4 2 8 6 6 5 2 7 7 8 7 4 4 4 (110)	7 6 5 5 7 5 4 5 5 4 4 6 4 7 5 8 6 5 5 5 (108)	12 14 12 7 14 12 8 7 13 10 10 11 6 14 12 16 13 9 9 9 (218)
	B_2	7 8 6 6 6 7 1 2 8 3 4 7 7 7 3 9 5 3 4 6 (109)	5 9 7 3 5 4 9 2 4 3 2 6 6 5 3 10 5 3 8 4 (103)	12 17 13 9 11 11 10 4 12 6 6 13 13 12 6 19 10 6 12 10 (212)
	B_3	7 5 6 7 5 5 3 4 6 7 7 5 5 7 3 5 4 6 6 8 (111)	6 9 8 7 6 5 2 7 9 7 9 7 5 7 7 6 7 7 7 10 (138)	13 14 14 14 11 10 5 11 15 14 16 12 10 14 10 11 11 13 13 18 (249)
	Total $(B_1+B_2+B_3)$	19 21 19 15 18 19 8 8 22 16 17 17 14 21 13 22 16 13 14 18 (330)	18 24 20 15 18 14 15 14 18 14 15 19 15 19 15 24 18 15 20 19 (349)	*Pupil totals* 37 45 39 30 36 33 23 22 40 30 32 36 29 40 28 46 34 28 34 37 (679)

significance of all effects involving occasions (C), since all the expectations for these effects involve only $\sigma^2_{PC.AB}$ plus the component specific to the effect itself. Similarly, the pupils mean square (from P, with $A \times B$) is the correct error term for testing the significance of the three effects based solely on the scores of different pupils, i.e. frame size (A), intelligence (B) and the $A \times B$ interaction. The F ratios in the last section were derived from this basis.

7.3 A double crossing of the nested factor

In the previous experiment the nested factor (pupils) was crossed with *one* other effect (occasions). It is possible, however, for the nested factor to be crossed with two or more effects. The following experiment provides an illustration of it being crossed with two other factors.

Table 7.5 (continued)

		A_1	A_2	*Total* (A_1+A_2)
C_2	B_1	7 6 9 3 7 3 4 4 2 6 6 4 4 6 4 5 5 4 4 9 (102)	5 5 5 3 7 7 2 4 2 8 7 7 5 5 5 5 1 4 7 5 (99)	12 11 14 6 14 10 6 8 4 14 13 11 9 11 9 10 6 8 11 14 (201)
	B_2	9 4 7 6 6 4 1 4 2 6 6 5 5 4 3 4 3 6 5 9 (99)	4 7 4 4 6 5 1 1 0 6 8 5 6 3 3 4 2 8 9 5 (92)	13 11 11 10 12 9 2 5 2 12 14 10 11 7 6 8 5 15 14 14 (191)
	B_3	9 7 6 4 2 4 5 6 6 6 6 7 4 4 5 5 4 6 3 8 (107)	7 8 6 4 4 6 5 1 6 8 7 5 5 3 6 4 5 8 4 10 (112)	16 15 12 8 6 10 10 7 12 14 13 12 9 7 11 9 9 14 7 18 (219)
	Total $(B_1+B_2+B_3)$	25 17 22 13 15 11 10 14 10 18 18 16 13 13 12 14 12 16 12 26 (308)	16 20 15 11 17 18 8 6 8 22 22 17 16 11 14 13 8 21 20 20 (303)	*Pupil totals* 41 37 37 24 32 29 18 20 18 40 40 33 29 25 26 27 20 37 32 46 (611)

Totals

A_1	638
A_2	652

B_1	419
B_2	403
B_3	468

C_1	679
C_2	611

Overall total = 1,290

N.B. Each of the twelve cells in C_1 contains the scores of the same twenty pupils in the same order; similarly for the twelve cells in C_2. The total for each cell is shown circled.

Key: A_1–Physical science; A_2–Biological science
B_1–Knowledge; B_2–Application; B_3–Evaluation
C_1–School 1; C_2–School 2

$P \times C$, within $A \times B$: $\sigma^2_{PC.AB}$

P, within $A \times B$: $\sigma^2_{PC.AB} + c\sigma^2_{P.AB}$

$A \times B \times C$: $\sigma^2_{PC.AB} + p\sigma^2_{ABC}$

$B \times C$: $\sigma^2_{PC.AB} + \cancel{p\sigma^2_{ABC}} + pa\sigma^2_{BC}$

$A \times C$: $\sigma^2_{PC.AB} + \cancel{p\sigma^2_{ABC}} + pb\sigma^2_{AC}$

$A \times B$: $\sigma^2_{PC.AB} + c\sigma^2_{P.AB} + \cancel{p\sigma^2_{ABC}} + pc\sigma^2_{AB}$

(Note that AB is involved in the subscript combination $P.AB$, so the component $c\sigma^2_{P.AB}$ now enters into the mean-square expectation for the first time since the second line above.)

C: $\sigma^2_{PC.AB} + \cancel{p\sigma^2_{ABC}} + \cancel{pa\sigma^2_{BC}} + \cancel{pb\sigma^2_{AC}} + pab\sigma^2_{C}$

B: $\sigma^2_{PC.AB} + c\sigma^2_{P.AB} + \cancel{p\sigma^2_{ABC}} + \cancel{pa\sigma^2_{BC}} + \cancel{pc\sigma^2_{AB}} + pac\sigma^2_{B}$

(Note that $c\sigma^2_{P.AB}$ appears, as it contains the subscript B, and is not deleted despite the fixedness of A.)

A: $\sigma^2_{PC.AB} + c\sigma^2_{P.AB} + \cancel{p\sigma^2_{ABC}} + \cancel{pb\sigma^2_{AC}} + \cancel{pc\sigma^2_{AB}} + pbc\sigma^2_{A}$

(Similarly, $c\sigma^2_{P.AB}$ again appears, and is not deleted.)

Two tests, one of physical science and one of biological science, were constructed, each being structured into subtests testing (a) knowledge (of specific facts, terminology, general principles, etc.), (b) the application of knowledge (in problems, new situations, etc.) and (c) the evaluation and scientific interpretation of data. There were therefore six subtests, which were separated on the basis of both subject matter (physical science and biology) and of objectives (knowledge, application and evaluation). The six subtests were administered to random samples of pupils—of the age group or attainment level for which they were designed—in several schools. The experiment was then a four-way experiment, in that each score could be classified in four ways, as belonging to a particular subject (A), objective (B), school (C) and pupil (P). Within each school the scores of the same pupils appear in all the cross-classifications of subject and objective. The factor of pupils, in other words, is nested within schools, but within each school is crossed with both subjects and objectives. Test scores for groups of twenty pupils in each of two schools are set out in table 7.5.

We see from table 7.5 that if the nested factor were ignored, the data would comprise that from a $2 \times 3 \times 2$ factorial experiment, subjects (A), objectives (B) and schools (C) being the three factors. We may begin, therefore, by separating the sum of squares for between cells into sums for the main effects A, B and C, for the three first-order interactions $A \times B$, $A \times C$ and $B \times C$ and the one second-order interaction $A \times B \times C$ between these effects. The calculation of these sums of squares follows precisely the pattern described in sections 6.2 and 7.2, and is not repeated here. The sums of squares are recorded in table 7.6.

Account must then be taken of the nested factor, pupils, and this has to be done in three distinct ways. First, there is a sum of squares for the differences between pupils (the differences between the pupil totals recorded in table 7.5) within each school. Secondly, there is a sum of squares for the interaction between pupils and subjects (a sum based on the differences between the $B_1+B_2+B_3$ totals of table 7.5) within each school. Thirdly, there is a sum of squares for the interaction between pupils and objectives (a sum based on the differences between the A_1+A_2 totals of table 7.5) within each school. If, finally, these three sums of squares are subtracted from the within-cells sum of squares, a residual sum—actually the sum of squares for the second-order interaction pupils × subjects × objectives within each school—would be obtained. The pattern of the calculation is set out below.

1. Total sum of squares $= \underbrace{(5^2+8^2+ \cdots +20^2)}_{\text{Sum of 240 terms}} - \dfrac{1{,}290 \times 1{,}290}{240}$

$= 7{,}878{\cdot}00 - 6{,}933{\cdot}75$

$= 944{\cdot}25$

2. Between-cells sum of squares $= \underbrace{\left(\dfrac{110^2}{20}+\dfrac{108^2}{20}+ \cdots +\dfrac{112^2}{20}\right)}_{\text{Sum of 12 terms}} - \dfrac{1{,}290^2}{240}$

$= 7{,}004{\cdot}10 - 6{,}933{\cdot}75$

$= 70{\cdot}35$

3. Within-cells sum of squares $= 944{\cdot}25 - 70{\cdot}35$

$= 873{\cdot}90$

4. | 10. Partitioning of the between-cells sum of squares into sums of squares for A, B, C, $A \times B$, $A \times C$, $B \times C$ and $A \times B \times C$ (procedure the same as that shown in section 6.2).

11. Between-pupils (P) (within C) sum of squares

$$= \underbrace{\left(\frac{37^2}{6}+\frac{45^2}{6}+\cdots+\frac{37^2}{6}\right)}_{\text{Sum of 20 terms}}{}^{*} - \frac{679^2}{120}$$

$$+ \underbrace{\left(\frac{41^2}{6}+\frac{37^2}{6}+\cdots+\frac{46^2}{6}\right)}_{\text{Sum of 20 terms}} - \frac{611^2}{120}$$

$$= 349{\cdot}65$$

12. Pupils (P) × subject (A) (within C) sum of squares

$$= \underbrace{\left(\frac{19^2}{3}+\frac{21^2}{3}+\cdots+\frac{19^2}{3}\right)}_{\text{Sum of 40 terms}} - \frac{679^2}{120}$$

$$- \left[\underbrace{\left(\frac{37^2}{6}+\frac{45^2}{6}+\cdots+\frac{37^2}{6}\right)}_{\text{Sum of 20 terms}} - \frac{679^2}{120}\right]$$

$$- \left(\frac{330^2}{60}+\frac{349^2}{60}-\frac{679^2}{120}\right)^{\dagger}$$

+A similar set of terms from the $B_1+B_2+B_3$ totals in C_2

$$= 108{\cdot}78$$

13. Pupils (P) × objectives (B) (within C) sum of squares

$$= \underbrace{\left(\frac{12^2}{2}+\frac{14^2}{2}+\cdots+\frac{18^2}{2}\right)}_{\text{Sum of 60 terms}} - \frac{679^2}{120}$$

$$- \left[\underbrace{\left(\frac{37^2}{6}+\frac{45^2}{6}+\cdots+\frac{37^2}{6}\right)}_{\text{Sum of 20 terms}} - \frac{679^2}{120}\right]$$

* The denominator of 6 is necessary, since each pupil total is the sum of six subtest scores; similarly for the denominators in the following two sums of squares (12 and 13).

† The first line is the sum of squares for the $B_1+B_2+B_3$ totals in C_1 of table 7.5. From this sum we subtract a sum of squares for both the main effects involved, that for pupils (the second line) and that for subjects (the third line). The pupils (P) × objectives (B) (within C) sum of squares (13) is derived from the A_1+A_2 totals in a similar manner.

$$-\left(\frac{218^2}{40}+\frac{212^2}{40}+\frac{249^2}{40}-\frac{679^2}{120}\right)$$

+A similar set of terms from the A_1+A_2 totals in C_2

$= 270{\cdot}04$

14. Residual sum of squares ($P\times A\times B$ interaction, within C) $= 873{\cdot}90-349{\cdot}65-108{\cdot}78-270{\cdot}04$

$= 145{\cdot}43$

Table 7.6 Analysis of variance of the data in table 7.5

Source of variation	*Sum of squares*	*Degrees of freedom*	*Mean square*
A	0·82	1	0·83
B	28·67	2	14·33*
C	19·27	1	19·27
$A\times B$	14·41	2	7·20*
$A\times C$	2·39	1	2·39
$B\times C$	1·11	2	0·55
$A\times B\times C$	3·68	2	1·84
Pupils (P), within C	349·65	38	9·20†
$P\times A$, within C	108·78	38	2·86
$P\times B$, within C	270·04	76	3·55†
Residual ($P\times A\times B$), within C	145·43	76	1·91
Total	944·25	239	

* Significant at the 5-per-cent level.
† Significant at the 1-per-cent level.

The analysis of variance is shown in table 7.6. The degrees of freedom for pupils follow from there being twenty pupils, and hence 19 degrees of freedom for each of the two schools. Similarly, within each school the pupils × subjects interaction has $19\times 1 = 19$ degrees of freedom, and the pupils × objectives interaction $19\times 2 = 38$ degrees of freedom. The degrees of freedom for the residual sum also follow in this way, or again

K

they may be obtained by subtracting the degrees of freedom for the other three within-schools sources of variation from those for within cells.

The mean squares for the last four lines of table 7.6—the four within-schools sources of variation—provide the error terms for testing the significance of the other effects. Thus, both subjects (A) and the subjects × schools interaction ($A \times C$) are tested against the mean square for pupils × subjects ($P \times A$), within schools. (An explanation of the choice of error term is postponed until the next section.) Both these effects are clearly insignificant, the F ratios being less than unity. Again, both objectives (B) and the objectives × schools interaction ($B \times C$) are tested against the mean square for pupils × objectives ($P \times B$), within schools. (In other words, for each effect involving either A or B the appropriate error term is provided by the interaction of the effect with pupils within schools.) We have, therefore,

for B, $F = \dfrac{14{\cdot}33}{3{\cdot}55} = 4{\cdot}04$, which for 2 and 76 degrees of freedom is significant at the 5-per-cent level (statistical table 2A);

and for $B \times C$, $F = \dfrac{0{\cdot}55}{3{\cdot}55} < 1$, so that the objectives × schools interaction is not statistically significant.

The mean square for pupils (P) within schools is the appropriate error for testing the significance of the differences between schools (C). We have, therefore,

for C, $F = \dfrac{19{\cdot}27}{9{\cdot}20} = 2{\cdot}09$, which for 1 and 38 degrees of freedom is not significant at the 5-per-cent level (statistical table 2A).

Finally, the subjects × objectives interaction ($A \times B$) and the second-order subjects × objectives × schools interaction ($A \times B \times C$) are tested against the residual mean square. We have, therefore,

for $A \times B$, $F = \dfrac{7{\cdot}20}{1{\cdot}91} = 3{\cdot}77$, which for 2 and 76 degrees of freedom is significant at the 5-per-cent level (statistical table 2A);

and for $A \times B \times C$, $F = \dfrac{1{\cdot}84}{1{\cdot}91} < 1$, so that the second-order interaction is not statistically significant.

We may note, too, that the significance of each of the first three within-schools effects could also be tested against the residual mean square, though these tests are of little practical interest. (Real differences amongst pupils and of pupil interactions may usually be assumed.) Two of these effects prove to be significant at the 1-per-cent level, as indicated in table 7.6.

Table 7.7 Total scores for the $A \times B$ cross-classifications in table 7.5

	A_1	A_2
B_1	212	207
B_2	208	195
B_3	218	250

To interpret the significant subjects × objectives interaction, the total (or mean) scores in the six cross-classifications have to be compared. These are set out in table 7.7. We see that although for each of the first two objectives, knowledge and application, the score in physical science is the higher, for evaluation it is the score in biology which is the higher. Assuming that all the subtests have been properly standardized, we may conclude that in the two schools sampled an understanding of the evaluatory aspects of science is better in biology than in physics, whereas achievement in the other aspects of science is better in physics. Moreover, since the second-order interaction, subjects × objectives × schools, is *not* significant, this finding may be held to apply equally to each of the schools. Overall it is the differences between objectives (not subjects) which command attention. Thus, the main effect of objectives is significant, as is also the pupils × objectives interaction within schools.

7.4 The model for a double crossing of the nested factor

The model for the science experiment just described may be written as

$$x_{ijkl} = M+A_i+B_j+C_k+(AB)_{ij}+(AC)_{ik}+(BC)_{jk}+(ABC)_{ijk}+P_{kl} \\ +(PA)_{ikl}+(PB)_{jkl}+(PAB)_{ijkl}$$

Again, the first eight terms are the same as those of the model for the three-factor experiment of chapter 6 (section 6.3), though A now refers to subject, B to objective and C to school. P_{kl} is a component common to all the scores of pupil l in school k. $(PA)_{ikl}$ is a component resulting from the interaction between subject i and pupil l in school k, and $(PB)_{jkl}$ is similarly a component resulting from the interaction between objective j and pupil l in school k. Finally, $(PAB)_{ijkl}$ (the residual term) is a component resulting from the interaction between subject i, objective j and pupil l in school k. We note that the subscript l does not occur without the accompanying subscript k, since pupils are nested within schools. In the particular experiment described, i and k both take on the values 1 and 2, j the values 1, 2 and 3, while l runs from 1 to 20.

The components analysis is given in table 7.8. Again the dot notation is used, the dot preceding the factor (schools) within which pupils are nested. (Thus, $\sigma^2_{P.C}$ denotes the variance of pupils within schools, $\sigma^2_{PA.C}$ the variance of the interaction between pupils and subjects within schools, and so on.) The mean-square expectations are derived from the basic variation ($\sigma^2_{PAB.C}$) as before, i.e. on the initial assumption that all effects are random, deletions for the fixedness of effects being subsequently made (section 6.3). Subjects and objectives must obviously be regarded as fixed objects, and schools is also taken as a fixed effect. Pupils, on the other hand, is a random effect. The mean-square expectations would then be derived as shown below.

$P \times A \times B$, within C: $\sigma^2_{PAB.C}$

$P \times B$, within C: $\sigma^2_{PAB.C} + a\sigma^2_{PB.C}$

$P \times A$, within C: $\sigma^2_{PAB.C} + b\sigma^2_{PA.C}$

P, within C: $\sigma^2_{PAB.C} + \cancel{a\sigma^2_{PB.C}} + \cancel{b\sigma^2_{PA.C}} + ab\sigma^2_{P.C}$

$A \times B \times C$: $\sigma^2_{PAB.C} + p\sigma^2_{ABC}$

$B \times C$: $\sigma^2_{PAB.C} + a\sigma^2_{PB.C} + \cancel{p\sigma^2_{ABC}} + pa\sigma^2_{BC}$

(Note that BC is involved in the subscript combination $PB.C$, so the component $a\sigma^2_{PB.C}$ appears, and is not deleted since P is a random effect.)

$A \times C$: $\sigma^2_{PAB.C} + b\sigma^2_{PA.C} + \cancel{p\sigma^2_{ABC}} + pb\sigma^2_{AC}$

(Similarly, the component $b\sigma^2_{PA.C}$ appears and is not deleted.)

$A \times B$: $\sigma^2_{PAB.C} + \cancel{p\sigma^2_{ABC}} + pc\sigma^2_{AB}$

C: $\sigma^2_{PAB.C} + \cancel{a\sigma^2_{PB.C}} + \cancel{b\sigma^2_{PA.C}} + ab\sigma^2_{P.C} + \cancel{p\sigma^2_{ABC}} + \cancel{pa\sigma^2_{BC}} + \cancel{pb\sigma^2_{AC}} + pab\sigma^2_{C}$

B: $\sigma^2_{PAB.C}+a\sigma^2_{PB.C}+p\cancel{\sigma^2_{ABC}}+pa\cancel{\sigma^2_{BC}}+pc\cancel{\sigma^2_{AB}}+pac\sigma^2_B$

(Note that the component $a\sigma^2_{PB.C}$ is retained despite C being a fixed effect, since the subscript is not 'essential', i.e. it comes after the dot.)

A: $\sigma^2_{PAB.C}+b\sigma^2_{PA.C}+p\cancel{\sigma^2_{ABC}}+pb\cancel{\sigma^2_{AC}}+pc\cancel{\sigma^2_{AB}}+pbc\sigma^2_A$

(Similarly, the component $b\sigma^2_{PA.C}$ is retained.)

With the deletions indicated, the mean-square expectations then become those as shown in table 7.8. It follows, too, that the correct error terms for testing the significance of the various effects are those employed in the previous section. All the F ratios used (p. 146) were, in fact, derived from the components analysis of table 7.8.

Table 7.8 Components analysis for a four-factor experiment, one factor being nested and doubly crossed

Source of variation	*Degrees of freedom**	*Mean-square expectation†*
A	$a-1$	$\sigma^2_{PAB.C}+b\sigma^2_{PA.C}+pbc\sigma^2_A$
B	$b-1$	$\sigma^2_{PAB.C}+a\sigma^2_{PB.C}+pac\sigma^2_B$
C	$c-1$	$\sigma^2_{PAB.C}+ab\sigma^2_{P.C}+pab\sigma^2_C$
$A\times B$	$(a-1)(b-1)$	$\sigma^2_{PAB.C}+pc\sigma^2_{AB}$
$A\times C$	$(a-1)(c-1)$	$\sigma^2_{PAB.C}+b\sigma^2_{PA.C}+pb\sigma^2_{AC}$
$B\times C$	$(b-1)(c-1)$	$\sigma^2_{PAB.C}+a\sigma^2_{PB.C}+pa\sigma^2_{BC}$
$A\times B\times C$	$(a-1)(b-1)(c-1)$	$\sigma^2_{PAB.C}+p\sigma^2_{ABC}$
P, within C	$c(p-1)$	$\sigma^2_{PAB.C}+ab\sigma^2_{P.C}$
$P\times A$, within C	$c(p-1)(a-1)$	$\sigma^2_{PAB.C}+b\sigma^2_{PA.C}$
$P\times B$, within C	$c(p-1)(b-1)$	$\sigma^2_{PAB.C}+a\sigma^2_{PB.C}$
$P\times A\times B$, within C (residual)	$c(p-1)(a-1)(b-1)$	$\sigma^2_{PAB.C}$

* These are written for a levels of A, b levels of B, c levels of C and p levels of P within each of the c levels of C.

† A, B and C are regarded as fixed effects, and P as a random effect.

7.5 Further consideration of error terms

Notwithstanding the implications of a components analysis, there are times when the use of another mean square for error is justified. Suppose, for instance, that in another experiment of similar design to the science experiment the schools effect may be considered random. (In other words, we select pupils from a random sample of schools, in which case, of course, the number of schools would almost certainly be far greater than two.) This means that some of the deletions of components from the mean-square expectations set out on pp. 148–9 would not now apply. For instance, in the mean-square expectation for A the component $pb\sigma^2_{AC}$ would have to be retained, so that the appropriate error term for testing the significance of subject differences is no longer the mean square of the pupils × subjects interaction ($P \times A$) within schools. We see, in fact, that the error term must be the mean square of the subjects × schools interaction ($A \times C$). This is because $F = \dfrac{\text{Mean square for } A}{\text{Mean square for } A \times C}$ estimates $\dfrac{\sigma^2_{PAB.C} + b\sigma^2_{PA.C} + pb\sigma^2_{AC} + pbc\sigma^2_A}{\sigma^2_{PAB.C} + b\sigma^2_{PA.C} + pb\sigma^2_{AC}}$ which is greater than unity only if σ^2_A is non-zero. Nevertheless, if a pattern of results such as that of table 7.6 were again obtained, it would be more prudent to test school differences against the mean square for the pupils × subjects interaction ($P \times A$) within schools as before.

This is because the mean square for the subjects × schools interaction ($A \times C$) is below expectation: it has turned out to be less than that for the pupils × subjects interaction ($P \times A$) within schools. $\left(F = \dfrac{2{\cdot}39}{2{\cdot}86} < 1\right.$ despite the fact that $F = \dfrac{\text{Mean square for } A \times C}{\text{Mean square for } P \times A, \text{ within } C}$ estimates $\dfrac{\sigma^2_{PAB.C} + b\sigma^2_{PA.C} + pb^2_{AC}}{\sigma^2_{PAB.C} + b\sigma^2_{PA.C}}$ which cannot be less than unity, even if $\left.\sigma^2_{AC} = 0.\right)$ Significance tests based on the subjects × schools interaction mean square will then be unduly optimistic, i.e. 'significant' results will be obtained too frequently. The use of the pupils × schools interaction within schools mean square as the error term is then to be preferred.*

* Similar considerations would caution against the use of the mean square for the objectives × schools interaction ($B \times C$) as an error term when this turns out to be less than the mean square for the pupils × objectives interaction ($P \times B$) within schools—and also against the use of the mean square for the subjects × objectives × schools interaction ($A \times B \times C$) when this is less than the residual mean square ($P \times A \times B$) within schools.

A practice which may occasionally be justified, and which provides an error term other than that dictated by a components analysis, is the practice known as *pooling*. This consists of adding together two or more sums of squares and then dividing by the combined degrees of freedom. The following illustration from table 7.6 is convenient.

The pupils × subjects interaction ($P \times A$) within schools fails to attain significance at the 5-per-cent level.* Clearly a non-zero value for the component $\sigma^2_{PA.C}$ has not been established. If we now make the step (a questionable one) of assuming that this component is in fact zero, it follows that the mean square for the pupils × subjects interaction ($P \times A$) within schools and the residual mean square ($P \times A \times B$, within C) both estimate precisely the same parameter, $\sigma^2_{PAB.C}$. A better estimate of this, i.e. a more stable estimate in that it is based on a larger number of degrees of freedom, would then be forthcoming from combining the two sums of squares and degrees of freedom as follows:

$$\frac{108{\cdot}78 + 145{\cdot}43}{38 + 76} = \frac{254{\cdot}21}{114} = 2{\cdot}23$$

This pooled mean square would then replace the former estimate (1·91) as the error term in testing the significance of, for instance, the subjects × objectives interaction ($A \times B$).

Pooling in this way is justified only if there is no pupils × subjects interaction within schools, i.e. if $\sigma^2_{PA.C} = 0$, and it is extremely doubtful that this is in fact so. First, pupils usually react differently to different subjects, and a non-zero $\sigma^2_{PA.C}$ would be expected (though if subjects were basically similar and had been taught in the same way—as is possible with physical and biological science taught as part of a unified general science course—a zero $\sigma^2_{PA.C}$ might reasonably be hypothesized). Secondly, the obtained subjects × pupils interaction only narrowly fails to attain significance at the 5-per-cent level (and *is* significant at the 10-per-cent level). It would have been more reassuring if we had expected a zero $\sigma^2_{PA.C}$—if the obtained interaction had provided a F ratio far nearer unity.

Generally, then, we should conclude that the pooling of sums of squares to provide error terms based on larger numbers of degrees of freedom may be recommended only (a) if there are non-statistical grounds for expecting the relevant population interactions to be zero (or, at any rate, to be of

* $F = \dfrac{2{\cdot}86}{1{\cdot}91} = 1{\cdot}50$ (for 38 and 76 degrees of freedom), as against a ratio of 1·55 necessary for significance at the 5-per-cent level (statistical table 2A).

negligible importance), and (b) if such grounds are clearly supported by the obtained *F* ratios, i.e. they should fail to attain significance at a predetermined level (such as the 5-per-cent level), and preferably fail by more than a narrow margin. Confidence that the relevant interactions are zero, or as near zero as would make little practical difference, should be reinforced by the statistical evidence before pooling can be advised. A more detailed discussion of this problem is provided by Binder (1955). A paper by Paull (1950) might also prove helpful.

References

BINDER, A. (1955) 'The choice of an error term in analysis of variance designs,' *Psychometrika*, **20,** 29–50.

LEWIS, D. G. and GREGSON, A. (1965) 'The effects of frame size and intelligence on learning from a linear program,' *Programmed Learning*, **1,** 170–5.

LINDQUIST, E. F. (1956) *Design and Analysis of Experiments in Psychology and Education*, Boston, Mass.: Houghton Mifflin, pp. 281–4.

PAULL, A. E. (1950) 'On a preliminary test for pooling mean squares in the analysis of variance,' *Annals of Mathematical Statistics*, **21,** 539–56.

SCHULTZ, E. F. (1955) 'Rules of thumb for determining expectations of mean squares,' *Biometrics*, **11,** 123–35.

Chapter 8 Latin-square Designs

8.1 Restricting randomization

In chapter 5 designs with randomized blocks were described. The sole reason for forming blocks—on the basis of such measures as I.Q. and previous attainment—was that of reducing variability. The variability within blocks is considerably less than would be the case from measurements made from persons selected at random. Nevertheless, within each block randomization plays an unfettered role (see figure 4).

Sometimes a further restriction on randomization might be advantageous. Thus, in agricultural experiments where the effect of different treatments (fertilizers) has to be evaluated, the total land available is divided into plots by an equal number of rows and columns. Different treatments are then assigned to the plots, so that each treatment occurs once and only once in each row, and once and only once in each column. It follows that the number of treatments must be the same as the number of rows (or columns). It follows, too, that if the rows are thought of as corresponding to the blocks of a randomized-blocks design, the arrangement of treatments for the plots within each block can be random provided that the same treatment is not repeated in any column. With five rows and five columns, for instance, and with the numerals 1, 2, 3, 4 and 5 referring to the different treatments, one such arrangement might be as follows:

		Columns				
		i	ii	iii	iv	v
	i	1	2	3	4	5
	ii	4	5	1	3	2
Rows	iii	2	1	4	5	3
	iv	3	4	5	2	1
	v	5	3	2	1	4

The essence of this arrangement is that differences in natural soil fertility are balanced out in *two* directions simultaneously: differences from row to row and differences from column to column. The arrangement is known as a Latin-square design.* Randomization procedures for obtaining Latin squares are discussed by Fisher and Yates (1963).

Table 8.1 Mean scores of four groups on four word lists presented in four forms (Latin-square design)

		Word lists (A) 1	2	3	4	*Totals for B*
Groups (B)	1	(C_1) 10·2	(C_2) 10·7	(C_3) 8·4	(C_4) 11·0	40·3
	2	(C_2) 13·5	(C_4) 13·1	(C_1) 10·8	(C_3) 10·1	47·5
	3	(C_3) 10·6	(C_1) 9·3	(C_4) 8·5	(C_2) 11·9	40·3
	4	(C_4) 10·2	(C_3) 8·4	(C_2) 12·7	(C_1) 7·8	39·1
Totals for A		44·5	41·5	40·4	40·8	

Overall total = 167·2

Totals for C	
C_1	38·1
C_2	48·8
C_3	37·5
C_4	42·8

Key for forms: C_1–Dictation, C_2–Multiple-choice, C_3–Incorrect spelling, C_4–Completion

In educational research the different treatments might be the forms in which a certain skill or trait is tested, the columns might be different tests and the rows different individuals or groups. An illustration similar to a research by Nisbett (1939) is appropriate. Different forms of testing spelling are investigated. Thus, children could be asked to write down words from dictation, to correct a list of words incorrectly spelt, to choose the correct spelling from a number of alternatives (multiple-choice form), or to complete words with a 'framework' of letters supplied (completion form)—four forms in all. Four lists of words thought to be of about equal difficulty would then be prepared, and four groups of children selected for testing. Each group would have to spell the words on all the lists, and each

* This is because the treatments are often denoted not by numerals but by Latin letters, *A*, *B*, *C*, etc.

list would be presented in a different form; but the combination of list and form would be different for each group. The design would be a Latin square. A possible arrangement would be that shown in table 8.1.

We see that group 1 attempts list 1 from dictation, list 2 from the multiple-choice form, list 3 from incorrect spelling and list 4 from the completion form; that group 2 attempts list 1 from the multiple-choice form, list 2 from the completion form, list 3 from dictation and list 4 from incorrect spelling; and so on. Each treatment (C)—the form of the test—is administered to all the groups, and each list of words is also administered to all the groups. Again, each list of words is administered with all the treatments. Differences between both groups and lists of words are therefore eliminated from the differences between the treatments.

With the data of table 8.1, the breakdown of the variation would be as shown below. An important point is that sets of treatment totals can be extracted from the table as well as sets of totals for columns (A) and rows (B). Thus, the total for C_1 is obtained as

$$10{\cdot}2+10{\cdot}8+9{\cdot}3+7{\cdot}8 = 38{\cdot}1$$

Sums of squares for *lists* (A), *groups* (B) and *treatments* (C) are obtained, and these are all subtracted from the total sum of squares to give a *residual* sum of squares.

1. Total sum of squares $= \underbrace{10{\cdot}2^2+10{\cdot}7^2+\cdots+7{\cdot}8^2}_{\text{Sum of 16 terms}} - \dfrac{167{\cdot}5\times 167{\cdot}2}{16}$

$$= 1{,}792{\cdot}04-1{,}747{\cdot}24$$
$$= 44{\cdot}80$$

2. Between-lists (A) sum of squares $= \dfrac{44{\cdot}5^2}{4}+\dfrac{41{\cdot}5^2}{4}+\cdots+\dfrac{40{\cdot}8^2}{4}-\dfrac{167{\cdot}2^2}{16}$

$$= 1{,}749{\cdot}82-1{,}747{\cdot}24$$
$$= 2{\cdot}58$$

3. Between-groups (B) sum of squares $= \dfrac{40{\cdot}3^2}{4}+\dfrac{47{\cdot}5^2}{4}+\cdots+\dfrac{39{\cdot}1^2}{4}-\dfrac{167{\cdot}2^2}{16}$

$$= 1{,}758{\cdot}31-1{,}747{\cdot}24$$
$$= 11{\cdot}07$$

4. Between-treatments (C) sum of squares $= \frac{38{\cdot}1^2}{4}+\frac{48{\cdot}8^2}{4}+\cdots+\frac{42{\cdot}8^2}{4}-\frac{167{\cdot}2^2}{16}$
$= 1{,}767{\cdot}78-1{,}747{\cdot}24$
$= 20{\cdot}54$

5. Residual sum of squares $= 44{\cdot}80-2{\cdot}58-11{\cdot}07-20{\cdot}54$
$= 10{\cdot}61$

The sums for all three of A, B and C have 3 degrees of freedom (each effect having four levels) and the total sum has 15 degrees of freedom (being based on the scores). The residual sum therefore has $15-9 = 6$ degrees of freedom. In general with an $a \times a$ square each of the three effects would have $(a-1)$ degrees of freedom, the degrees of freedom for the residual sum being

$$a^2-1-(a-1)-(a-1)-(a-1) = a^2-3a+2 = (a-1)(a-2)$$

The analysis of variance is accordingly set out as in table 8.2. If the residual mean square could be accepted as a valid estimate of error, the treatment differences (C) would be tested by $F = \frac{6{\cdot}84}{1{\cdot}77} = 3{\cdot}86$, which for 3 and 6 degrees of freedom is not significant at the 5-per-cent level (statistical table 2A). The A and B differences could also be tested in this way if they happened to be of experimental interest. In this experiment they are not.

Table 8.2 Analysis of variance of the data in table 8.1

Source of variation	*Sum of squares*	*Degrees of freedom*	*Mean square*
A	2·58	3	
B	11·07	3	
C	20·54	3	6·84
Residual	10·61	6	1·77
Total	44·80	15	

The analysis is one based upon group means, and is therefore precisely the same as if the rows represented different individuals. If, however, the scores of the individual children of each group were considered, the total sum of squares would first be resolved into sums for *between cells* and *within cells* (see figure 5), the sums for lists, groups, treatments and residual then appearing as components of the former. The within-cells sum would also be resolved into separate components if the scores of the same group of persons appear in all the cells of any one row. The complete analysis is developed in section 8.2.

We may note, too, that the rows of the square differ not only by each having a different group but also because the *order* in which the treatments are presented is different. (It is assumed that all groups take the word lists in the order 1 2 3 4, the columns of the square.) Thus, group 1 takes the test forms in the order 1 2 3 4, group 2 in the order 2 4 1 3, and so on. Therefore, even if the groups happen to be exactly equal in spelling ability, a non-zero row effect must be expected. Again, whatever the actual group differences in spelling ability, differences arising from the order in which the test forms are taken will also be involved. In other words, the effect of order is confounded (or mixed in—see footnote p. 128) with that of groups. It is also confounded with that of word lists. A way of separating out the effect of order is described in section 8.5.

8.2 The model

We shall first describe the model for the Latin square when each cell consists of n scores, all the scores from any one cell being independent of those from any other. The model when there is only one score per cell (as is the case for the experiment described in section 8.1) then follows from putting $n = 1$. With the same notation as that used in previous designs, the model may be set down as

$$x_{ijkl} = M + A_i + B_j + C_k + R_{ijk} + e_{ijkl}$$

where M is a component common to all the scores;

A_i is a component common to all scores in level i of factor A, i.e. all scores of *column* i in an arrangement of data like that of table 8.1;

B_i is a component common to all scores in level j of factor B—or all scores in *row* j;

C_i is a component common to all scores in level k of factor C—or all scores in *treatment* k;

R_{ijk} is a component common to all scores in column i, row j and treatment k;

and e_{ijkl} is a component specific to the score of person l in column i, row j and treatment k.

Generally all three of i, j and k run from 1 to a (in the experiment described $a = 4$). The six contributions to the score x_{ijkl} are all independent of each other—and so, in particular, person l of any one cell is not the same person as person l of any other—and the As, Bs, Cs, Rs and es are regarded as being drawn from normally distributed populations with means of zero, and variances of σ_A^2, σ_B^2, σ_C^2, σ_R^2 and σ^2 respectively.

The components analysis is then as shown in table 8.3. We see that the residual (R) mean square provides the error term for testing the significance of each of the three main effects. The B effect could not be designated 'groups' as in the experiment of section 8.1 because the analysis presupposes separate, and independently selected, groups for each cell. B would have to be a characteristic common to all scores in each row, such as when the scores come from persons of the same level of motivation or I.Q.

Table 8.3 Components analysis for a Latin-square experiment, with independent groups in each cell

Source of variation	*Degrees of of freedom**	*Mean-square expectation*
A	$a-1$	$\sigma^2+n\sigma_R^2+an\sigma_A^2$
B	$a-1$	$\sigma^2+n\sigma_R^2+an\sigma_B^2$
C	$a-1$	$\sigma^2+n\sigma_R^2+an\sigma_C^2$
R	$(a-1)(a-2)$	$\sigma^2+n\sigma_R^2$
Within cells	$a^2(n-1)$	σ^2

* These are written for an $a \times a$ square with n scores in each cell.

If, as is often the case in practice, the scores from cells in the same row are not independent and are all obtained by the same group of n persons, the above model is inadequate. An additional component representing the element common to all scores obtained by the same person must appear. The model becomes

$$x_{ijkl} = M+A_i+B_j+C_k+R_{ijk}+P_{jl}+e_{ijkl}$$

where six of the terms have the same meaning as before, and where the additional term P_{jl} is a component common to all the scores of person l in row j. This component is regarded as coming from a normally distributed population with a mean of zero and a variance of σ_P^2. In accordance with the dot notation adopted in chapter 7, this variance will be represented by $\sigma_{P.B}^2$ showing that the persons (P) are nested within rows (B). $\sigma_{P.B}^2$ can, of course, be estimated independently of the other effects in precisely the same way as, for instance, the effect of pupils was estimated from the data of table 7.5 (see pp. 140–1). The components analysis is then as shown in table 8.4. The source of variance designated 'remainder' could also be described as the $P \times A$ interaction within B. Again we see that it is the residual mean square which provides the error term for testing the significance of the A and C effects. No test for the significance of the B effect is evident, but this would seldom be of interest anyhow. Usually the persons tested would be divided into groups (the rows of the square) at random, so that there would be no real row differences (i.e. $\sigma_B^2 = 0$).

Table 8.4 Components analysis for a Latin-square experiment, the same group being used for all cells in a row

Source of variation	*Degrees of freedom**	*Mean-square expectation*
A	$a-1$	$\sigma^2+n\sigma_R^2+an\sigma_A^2$
B (rows)	$a-1$	$\sigma^2+a\sigma_{P.B}^2+n\sigma_R^2+an\sigma_B^2$
C	$a-1$	$\sigma^2+n\sigma_R^2+an\sigma_C^2$
R	$(a-1)(a-2)$	$\sigma^2+n\sigma_R^2$
Persons P, within B	$a(n-1)$	$\sigma^2+a\sigma_{P.B}^2$
Remainder	$a(a-1)(n-1)$	σ^2

* These are written for an $a \times a$ square where persons are nested within rows (n in each row).

Note that if $n = 1$, the last line of table 8.3 and the last two lines of table 8.4 disappear (since the degrees of freedom become zero). The two tables become identical, in fact, as σ^2 and (in table 8.4) $\sigma_{P.B}^2$ must then be removed from all the mean-square expectations. σ_R^2 becomes the mean-square expectation of the residual and provides the error term for testing the A, B and C effects. We have already seen that the residual mean square is the appropriate error term for testing the A and C effects when groups not individuals constitute the rows (i.e. $n > 1$). The degrees of freedom on which the residual mean square is based, $(a-1)(a-2)$, is therefore of special interest.

With a 4×4 square the number of degrees of freedom for the residual is $3 \times 2 = 6$, and with a 3×3 square it is only $2 \times 1 = 2$. Obviously considerable instability must be expected in the residual mean square for Latin squares as small as these. As large squares are seldom practicable in educational research—since each addition to the row and column size must be matched by an additional treatment—the advantage of using, if possible, an error term based on a larger number of degrees of freedom is apparent. One way of increasing the number of degrees of freedom for error would be to use not a single square but several squares in combination. A second way (not dissimilar from the first) would be to use groups, not individuals, in the rows, and so secure a within-cells (table 8.3) or a remainder (table 8.4) mean square.

We see from the components analyses, however, that the A and C effects can be tested for significance by the within-cells or remainder mean square only if $\sigma_R^2 = 0$, i.e. only if there are no distinctive components for cells. In certain circumstances this assumption might not be unreasonable. These circumstances, however, must include an allocation of the treatments to the cells of the square *at random*—subject only to the requirements of the design (i.e. no treatment appearing twice in the same row or column). In particular, the treatments must not be allocated to the cells in any prescribed order. Latin squares in which this has been done are termed *systematic squares*. Examples of systematic squares are the diagonal square, which for five treatments would be written as

1	2	3	4	5
5	1	2	3	4
4	5	1	2	3
3	4	5	1	2
2	3	4	5	1

and the Knut Vick square

1	2	3	4	5
4	5	1	2	3
2	3	4	5	1
5	1	2	3	4
3	4	5	1	2

If squares such as these were deliberately chosen, the within-cells or—when the same groups are used throughout the rows—remainder mean square would not provide a valid estimate of error. Furthermore, even when individuals and not groups are represented by the rows of the square, a deliberate choice of a systematic square is inadvisable. This is because the R components of the model would not then constitute random errors. A discussion of this is provided by Fisher (1951).

8.3 Comparison with the factorial design

A practical advantage the Latin square enjoys over the factorial design is that far fewer combinations of factor levels are needed. Thus, with three factors each of four levels—which corresponds to the experiment described in section 8.1—the factorial design would require $4 \times 4 \times 4 = 64$ different combinations for testing, as against only sixteen for the Latin square. For the particular experiment of section 8.1 a factorial design would not be appropriate. It would require combining each word list with each form of testing with each group, which would mean that each group would be asked to spell the same words in four different forms of testing. This arrangement would undermine the experiment. A person's ability to spell certain words would inevitably be affected by being required to spell the same words before (in a different form of test). For many experiments, on the other hand, a factorial design would be practicable—provided, of course, that the number of levels of all three factors is the same, or could be made the same. The purpose would then be, not that of removing extraneous influences, but of evaluating the effect of factors of intrinsic interest. It is important to realize, however, that the advantage of the Latin square can be bought at too high a price.

The price to be paid can best be realized from comparing the model for the Latin square (pp. 157–8) with that for the three-factor experiment in chapter 6 (p. 117). We see at once that, compared with the model for the factorial design, the Latin square has all the interaction components missing. In other words, the Latin-square design *assumes* that all the interactions are zero. This assumption is necessary if only because there are simply not enough degrees of freedom available for separating out all the interactions that may exist. If any interactions do in fact exist, they are confounded with the main effects. Also, the residual mean square would not be a suitable error term for testing the significance of the main effects.

Let us suppose that in the experiment described in section 8.1 an appreciable $B \times C$ interaction exists, and that the interaction components are as shown below. (These correspond to the fourth entry in each of the cells of table 5.4. We note that they sum to zero in every row and column.)

	C_1	C_2	C_3	C_4
B_1	5	0	−2	−3
B_2	−2	7	−4	−1
B_3	4	−2	−1	−1
B_4	−7	−5	7	5

The Latin square for the experiment is as follows (see table 8.1).

	A_1	A_2	A_3	A_4
B_1	C_1	C_2	C_3	C_4
B_2	C_2	C_4	C_1	C_3
B_3	C_3	C_1	C_4	C_2
B_4	C_4	C_3	C_2	C_1

Consider the A effect, that based solely on the differences among the column sums. Each column sum is the sum of four cells as set out below.

Column 1	*Column* 2	*Column* 3	*Column* 4
$A_1B_1C_1$	$A_2B_1C_2$	$A_3B_1C_3$	$A_4B_1C_4$
$+A_1B_2C_2$	$+A_2B_2C_4$	$+A_3B_2C_1$	$+A_4B_2C_3$
$+A_1B_3C_3$	$+A_2B_3C_1$	$+A_3B_3C_4$	$+A_4B_3C_2$
$+A_1B_4C_4$	$+A_2B_4C_3$	$+A_3B_4C_2$	$+A_4B_4C_1$

The sums are obviously balanced with respect to both the B and the C effects separately, since each of the Bs and Cs enter once, and only once, into each sum. In other words, each of the B and C effects acts independently of A. The sums are not balanced, however, with respect to the interaction of B and C; this is evident if we write in the possible interaction components specified above. (See the top of p. 163.) It follows, therefore, that with a $B \times C$ interaction considerable differences can exist among the column sums, even if A_1, A_2, A_3 and A_4 do not differ in their effect at each of the levels of B or C separately. The $B \times C$ interaction, in other words, is confounded with the A effect.

In the same way it can be shown that the $A \times C$ interaction is con-

Column 1	*Column* 2	*Column* 3	*Column* 4
$\overbrace{A_1B_1C_1}^{5}$	$\overbrace{A_2B_1C_2}^{0}$	$\overbrace{A_3B_1C_3}^{-2}$	$\overbrace{A_4B_1C_4}^{-3}$
$+\overbrace{A_1B_2C_2}^{7}$	$+\overbrace{A_2B_2C_4}^{-1}$	$+\overbrace{A_3B_2C_1}^{-2}$	$+\overbrace{A_4B_2C_3}^{-4}$
$+\overbrace{A_1B_3C_3}^{-1}$	$+\overbrace{A_2B_3C_1}^{4}$	$+\overbrace{A_3B_3C_4}^{-1}$	$+\overbrace{A_4B_3C_2}^{-2}$
$+\overbrace{A_1B_4C_4}^{5}$	$+\overbrace{A_2B_4C_3}^{7}$	$+\overbrace{A_3B_4C_2}^{-5}$	$+\overbrace{A_4B_4C_1}^{-7}$
$5+7-1+5 = 16$	$0-1+4+7 = 10$	$-2-2-1-5 = -10$	$-3-4-2-7 = -16$

founded with the B effect, and that the $A \times B$ interaction is confounded with the C effect. It can be shown, too, that the second-order interaction $A \times B \times C$ is confounded with each of the A, B and C effects. If zero interactions are *not* assumed, the mean-square expectations for the Latin-square design will in fact be as given in table 8.5. (See Wilk and Kempthorne 1957 for a detailed discussion.) These are written for a mixed model with the rows effect (B) random and the columns (A) and treatment (C) effects fixed. If the rows effect is also fixed, then the component σ^2_{AB} must be deleted from the mean-square expectation of A, and the component σ^2_{BC} deleted from the mean-square expectation of C. Obviously if all these interactions exist, no valid tests of significance are possible.

Latin squares are used extensively in agricultural research, since there interactions are not a serious issue. In field experiments, for instance, a row by column interaction would arise if there was a fertility gradient *not* parallel to the sides of the square. Provided that reasonably large squares (at least 5×5 squares, say) are used—where the distorting effects of any interactions would be less than with smaller squares—and systematic squares are avoided—except in so far as these might arise occasionally from a random arrangement of the treatments—no serious objection to the use of Latin squares could be sustained. In educational research, however, the situation is very different. First, large squares are seldom used. Secondly, we should note that, whereas the agricultural worker effects a double (row and column) control over a *single* extraneous influence (soil variability), the educational researcher seeks to control *two essentially different* influences. The interactions may then be much more marked. Only if the investigator has grounds for believing the interactions to be negligible should the Latin-square design be used.

Table 8.5 Components analysis for a Latin-square experiment with independent groups in each cell when zero interactions are not assumed

Source of variation	*Degrees of of freedom**	*Mean-square expectation*
A	$a-1$	$\sigma^2+n\sigma_R^2+\left(1-\frac{2}{a}\right)\sigma_{ABC}^2+\sigma_{AB}^2+\sigma_{BC}^2+a\sigma_A^2$
B	$a-1$	$\sigma^2+n\sigma_R^2+\left(1-\frac{1}{a}\right)\sigma_{ABC}^2+\sigma_{AC}^2+a\sigma_B^2$
C	$a-1$	$\sigma^2+n\sigma_R^2+\left(1-\frac{2}{a}\right)\sigma_{ABC}^2+\sigma_{AB}^2+\sigma_{BC}^2+a\sigma_C^2$
R	$(a-1)(a-2)$	$\sigma^2+n\sigma_R^2+\left(1-\frac{2}{a}\right)\sigma_{ABC}^2+\sigma_{AB}^2+\sigma_{BC}^2+\sigma_{AC}^2$
Within cells	$a^2(n-1)$	σ^2

* These are written for an $a \times a$ square with n scores in each cell.

In the experiment on spelling, for instance, the use of the Latin square would be justified only if we could be sure that no appreciable interaction exists between the word lists and the test forms, between the groups and the word lists, and between the groups and the test forms. It would be preferable, too, for any investigator's 'hunch' that all these interactions are negligible to be supported by some empirical evidence. If such evidence is not available, the factorial design, if practicable, is to be preferred.

8.4 The 2×2 square

The 2×2 square stands on its own in so far as the residual effect now disappears. This is because there are no degrees of freedom available. We

Table 8.6 Scores of two groups on two test forms presented on two occasions (change-over design)

		Occasions 1		*Occasions* 2		*Person totals*	*Totals*
Groups	1	33		39		72	
		25		28		53	
		30	I	30	II	60	
		31		36		67	
		34	(153)	37	(170)	71	323
	2	30		31		61	
		25		29		54	
		37	II	34	I	71	
		32		32		64	
		32	(156)	34	(160)	66	316
Totals		309		330			639

Totals of forms

Form	Total
I	313
II	326

N.B. (a) The two scores in each row belong to the same person.
(b) The four cell totals are shown circled.

Key: I – Form 1 of test II – Form 2 of test

---

have seen that in an $a \times a$ square the degrees of freedom for the residual sum of squares are $(a-1)(a-2)$, and when $a = 2$ this becomes zero. This links up with the fact that only two arrangements of treatments are possible, i.e. $\begin{bmatrix} 1 & 2 \\ 2 & 1 \end{bmatrix}$ and $\begin{bmatrix} 2 & 1 \\ 1 & 2 \end{bmatrix}$ and if one of these arrangements yields a certain treatment sum of squares, the second arrangement will then necessarily yield the same treatment sum of squares, too. The 3 degrees of freedom between cells are fully accounted for by the single degree of freedom for each of the rows, columns and treatments.

The 2×2 square is, nevertheless, useful when it is groups and not individuals who constitute the rows. (Alternatively, a series of squares with individuals constituting rows could be used.) A frequent use of the square in educational research is that of determining a difference in difficulty between two tests, and more especially between two parallel forms of the same test. One group of children would take form 1 followed by form 2, and a second group form 2 followed by form 1. The effect of practice—the increase in score to be expected on the form taken second—would then be removed in a comparison of the forms from the two groups combined. We might, of course, be interested in the practice effect also. This would be obtained from a comparison of the total score on the forms taken second—forms 1 and 2 combined—with that on the forms taken first. Since the order of the test forms changes for the second group, this design is referred to as a *change-over* (also a *cross-over*) design.

Suppose that with five persons in each group (in an actual experiment the number would be considerably larger) the test scores are as shown in table 8.6. The analysis would, in the first place, partition the total sum of squares into sums for between cells and within cells. The former sum would then be divided into sums of squares for occasions of testing (columns), groups (rows) and treatments (test forms 1 and 2). Since within each group the scores in the two cells are not independent, a pair of scores (one on each occasion) being derived from the same person, a sum of squares for between persons within groups must be extracted from the within-cells sum (see table 8.4). The remaining part of the within-cells sum is the persons $\times$ occasions interaction within groups. The calculation is as shown below.

1. Total sum of squares

$$= \underbrace{(33^2+25^2+\cdots+34^2)}_{\text{Sum of 20 terms}}-\frac{639\times 639}{20}$$

$$= 20{,}681-20{,}416{\cdot}05$$

$$= 264{\cdot}95$$

2. Between-cells sum of squares

$$= \left(\frac{153^2}{5}+\frac{170^2}{5}+\cdots+\frac{160^2}{5}\right)-\frac{639^2}{20}$$

$$= 20{,}449-20{,}416{\cdot}05$$

$$= 32{\cdot}95$$

3. Within-cells sum of squares $= 264{\cdot}95 - 32{\cdot}95$
$= 232{\cdot}00$

4. Between-occasions (A) sum of squares $\left.\right\} = \dfrac{309^2}{10} + \dfrac{330^2}{10} - \dfrac{639^2}{20}$
$= 20{,}438{\cdot}10 - 20{,}416{\cdot}05$
$= 22{\cdot}05$

5. Between-groups (B) sum of squares $\left.\right\} = \dfrac{323^2}{10} + \dfrac{316^2}{10} - \dfrac{639^2}{20}$
$= 20{,}418{\cdot}50 - 20{,}416{\cdot}05$
$= 2{\cdot}45$

6. Between-forms (C) sum of squares $\left.\right\} = \dfrac{313^2}{10} + \dfrac{326^2}{10} - \dfrac{639^2}{20}$
$= 20{,}424{\cdot}50 - 20{,}416{\cdot}05$
$= 8{\cdot}45$

(Note that these last three sums combine to give the between-cells sum, 32·95.)

7. Between persons (P), within groups sum of squares

$$= \underbrace{\left(\frac{72^2}{2} + \frac{53^2}{2} + \cdots + \frac{71^2}{2}\right)}_{\text{Sum of 5 terms}} - \frac{323^2}{10}$$

$$+ \underbrace{\left(\frac{61^2}{2} + \frac{54^2}{2} + \cdots + \frac{66^2}{2}\right)}_{\text{Sum of 5 terms}} - \frac{316^2}{10}$$

$= 208{\cdot}00$

8. Remainder sum of squares ($P \times A$ interaction, within B) $\left.\right\} = 232{\cdot}00 - 208{\cdot}00$
$= 24{\cdot}00$

The between-persons sum has 8 degrees of freedom (4 from each group), and the residual sum also has 8 degrees of freedom ($4 \times 1 = 4$ from each group), giving together the 16 degrees of freedom for within cells. All the sums of squares and degrees of freedom are set out in table 8.7. The effect of both occasions (A) and test forms (C) are tested for significance against the residual mean square, since differences between the two occasions and between the two test forms are based on scores from the same persons (see also the components analysis, table 8.4). For occasions, therefore, we have

$$F = \frac{22{\cdot}05}{3{\cdot}00} = 7{\cdot}35$$

which, for 1 and 8 degrees of freedom, is significant at the 5-per-cent level (statistical table 2A). For test forms we have

$$F = \frac{8{\cdot}45}{3{\cdot}00} = 2{\cdot}82$$

which, for 1 and 8 degrees of freedom, is not significant at the 5-per-cent level. Of course, the obtained difference in mean score, though not significant, might still be of practical importance.

Table 8.7 Analysis of variance of the data in table 8.6

Source of variation	*Sum of squares*	*Degrees of freedom*	*Mean square*
A	22·05	1	22·05
B	2·45	1	
C	8·45	1	8·45
Persons (P), within B	208·00	8	
$P \times A$, within B	24·00	8	3·00
Total	264·95	19	

We would usually have no interest in the group differences themselves. In experiments of this kind the persons tested are separated into two groups at random, in which case no real group difference exists, i.e. the component σ_B^2 of table 8.4 is zero. The component σ_R^2 shown in table 8.4 is also zero, since the residual source of variation does not now exist. Lines 2 and 4 of table 8.7 could then be combined to give a single source of variation for persons.

Source of variation	*Sum of squares*	*Degrees of freedom*
B	2·45	1
Persons (P), within B	208·00	8
P	210·45	9

8.5 Extensions of the Latin square

The principle of restricting the randomization of treatments within a Latin square can be carried one or more stages further. One additional restriction upon the randomization might, for instance, be imposed. This would result in three, not two, distinct sources of variation being equalized. The number of classifications of the additional source—or the number of levels of the new factor—must be the same as the number of treatments, i.e. the number of rows (or columns) in the square. Each treatment would then occur once and only once with each of the additional classifications, as well as once and only once in each row and column of the square. Such an arrangement is termed a *Graeco-Latin square.**

In the 4×4 square of section 8.1 the treatments were denoted by C_1, C_2, C_3 and C_4. If we then use the letter D for the additional classifications, an example of a Graeco-Latin square would be

C_1D_1	C_2D_2	C_3D_3	C_4D_4
C_3D_4	C_4D_3	C_1D_2	C_2D_1
C_4D_2	C_3D_1	C_2D_4	C_1D_3
C_2D_3	C_1D_4	C_4D_1	C_3D_2

We note that each of the Cs occurs once and only once with each of the Ds, and each of the Ds (as well as the Cs) occurs once and only once in each row and column. The square could, in fact, be regarded as the result of two Latin squares being superimposed, the squares

C_1	C_2	C_3	C_4
C_3	C_4	C_1	C_2
C_4	C_3	C_2	C_1
C_2	C_1	C_4	C_3

and

D_1	D_2	D_3	D_4
D_4	D_3	D_2	D_1
D_2	D_1	C_4	D_3
D_3	D_4	D_1	D_2

(Squares which can be superimposed in this manner are called 'orthogonal' Latin squares.)

To develop the illustration of the Latin square in section 8.1, in which the columns of the square represent word lists, the rows groups, and the

* The additional classifications are often denoted by Greek letters (α, β, γ, etc.), which are then used in combination with Latin letters for the original square. Hence the name Graeco-Latin square.

Cs forms of testing, the new classification *D* could now represent the *order* in which the different combinations of word lists and test forms are presented. Thus, in the above Graeco-Latin square group 1 (in row 1) would take list 1 in form 1 first, list 2 in form 2 second, list 3 in form 3 third, and list 4 in form 4 fourth. Again, group 2 (in row 2) would take list 4 in form 2 first (since C_2D_1 is in column 4 of the square), list 3 in form 1 second (since C_1D_2 is in column 3), list 2 in form 4 third, and list 1 in form 3 fourth; and similarly for groups 3 and 4. The result would be an exact balancing of differences of order, as well as those of word lists and groups, in a comparison of test forms, the *Cs*. Differences of order would also be balanced out in a comparison of word lists and (should the comparison be of any interest) of groups.

We saw that in the 4×4 Latin square there were 6 degrees of freedom available for the residual (table 8.2). In the 4×4 Graeco-Latin square 3 of these degrees of freedom will be taken over by the additional classification *D*. Generally for an $a \times a$ square the degrees of freedom will separate as follows:

A	$a-1$
B	$a-1$
C	$a-1$
D	$a-1$
Residual	$(a-1)(a-3)$

For a 4×4 square there would be only $3 \times 1 = 3$ degrees of freedom available for the residual, and for a 3×3 square there will be no degrees of freedom available at all. (A 2×2 Graeco-Latin square, of course, cannot even exist!) Obviously for small squares it is highly desirable that groups and not individuals be tested in the rows, or else that a combination of several Graeco-Latin squares be used. Again, systematic squares should be avoided as an automatic choice. The components analysis of a Graeco-Latin-square experiment follows the pattern of tables 8.3 and 8.4 with an additional line for the new source of variation *D* appearing (the mean-square expectation for *D* being similar to that for *A* and *C*), and with $(a-1)(a-3)$ replacing $(a-1)(a-2)$ as the number of degrees of freedom for the residual *R*.

Graeco-Latin squares have been constructed for all numbers of treatments from three to twelve with the exception of six and ten. They also exist for all odd numbers of treatments. Examples of Graeco-Latin squares for up to twelve treatments are given by Cochran and Cox (1957). With regard to their usefulness in educational research, it must be borne in mind that they are subject to all the disadvantages of Latin squares. In particular, each main effect would be confounded with the first-order interactions of all the other effects, and also with the higher-order interactions.

The principle of equalizing an additional source of variation among the treatments could, in theory, be carried further. Thus, a fourth source of variation E could be simultaneously controlled, given that the number of classifications of E is the same as the number of treatments. Again, each classification of E would occur once and only once in each row and column of the square, and once and only once with each of the C and D classifications. Such an arrangement is termed a *hyper-Graeco-Latin square*. An example for a 4×4 square is shown below. We may note that the 15 degrees of freedom for between cells is now fully accounted for by the 3 degrees of freedom for each of A (rows), B (columns), C, D and E. (It follows, then, that if the rows represent individuals, a single 4×4 square is of little value; a combination of several squares would be needed.)

$C_1D_1E_1$	$C_2D_2E_2$	$C_3D_3E_3$	$C_4D_4E_4$
$C_3D_4E_2$	$C_4D_3E_1$	$C_1D_2E_4$	$C_2D_1E_3$
$C_4D_2E_3$	$C_3D_1E_4$	$C_2D_4E_1$	$C_1D_3E_2$
$C_2D_3E_4$	$C_1D_4E_3$	$C_4D_1E_2$	$C_3D_2E_1$

The writer knows of no instance where such squares have been fruitfully applied in the field of education.

References

COCHRAN, W. G. and COX, G. M. (1957) *Experimental Designs*, New York: Wiley (2nd edition), pp. 146–7.

FISHER, R. A. (1951) *The Design of Experiments*, Edinburgh: Oliver & Boyd (6th edition), pp. 74–8.

FISHER, R. A. and YATES, F. (1963) *Statistical Tables for Biological, Agricultural and Medical Research*, Edinburgh: Oliver & Boyd (6th edition).

NISBETT, S. D. (1939) 'Non-dictated spelling tests,' *British Journal of Educational Psychology*, **9**, 29–44.

WILK, M. B. and KEMPTHORNE, O. (1957) 'Non-additivities in a Latin-square design,' *Journal of the American Statistical Association*, **52**, 218–36.

Chapter 9 Covariance Designs

9.1 Statistical control

In the randomized-blocks design described in chapter 5, differences resulting from a factor extraneous to the treatments studied were controlled. Blocks could be formed on the basis of, say, intelligence, so that all the persons in any one block were within the same (narrow) intelligence range. The results were then affected to but a small extent by differences in intelligence.

A practical disadvantage in controlling intelligence experimentally in this way is that the score of each person on a suitable test must be known beforehand. Again, many of the persons available for the experiment might not have scores or I.Q.s falling conveniently into the blocks, so that some of the information available (or potentially available) would be sacrificed. Sometimes, too, it might not be advisable or even possible to control an extraneous factor by forming blocks at the beginning of the experiment. Such a situation would arise, for instance, in an investigation into the effectiveness of different methods of studying. The length of time each person spends studying could not realistically be fixed beforehand. This leads us to the possibility of controlling differences in the extraneous factor (intelligence, length of time studying, etc.) in another way. One such way is provided by the *analysis of covariance*. The control is exercised statistically rather than experimentally.

In the methods experiment, for example, with intelligence as the extraneous factor, we would begin by considering the connection between final attainment and intelligence *within each method group*. In particular, the regression of attainment on intelligence would be determined. This regression—essentially a measure of average increase in attainment for a unit increase in intelligence—would differ from group to group. But it might well be that these differences in regression would be small, or at any rate statistically insignificant. If so, *one* population regression could be assumed for all the groups. This would be estimated from an average of all the separate within-groups regressions, and would then be applied to the differences in mean scores (attainment and intelligence mean scores) of the groups.

If, for instance, one group were superior in intelligence—its intelligence mean score being above the overall intelligence mean—the extent of the corresponding superiority expected in attainment could be determined. This expected superiority would depend solely on the group's intelligence mean expressed as a deviation from the overall mean, and the regression of attainment on intelligence. If the extent of this expected superiority were then subtracted from the group's actual attainment mean, the attainment mean would be *adjusted* for the difference in intelligence. Again, if another group were inferior in intelligence, the extent of the corresponding inferiority expected in its attainment would be determined. This amount would then be added to the group's actual attainment mean to give a mean adjusted for the difference in intelligence.

When the actual attainments of all the groups have been adjusted in this way, it may be found that the rank order of adjusted means differs considerably from that of the obtained means. For instance, a group with a markedly inferior average intelligence would merit a substantial 'adjustment', and with only an average actual attainment would end up with a high adjusted attainment. Similarly, a group with high intelligence but only an average attainment would necessarily have an adjusted attainment well below average.

Another possibility is that, whereas the actual group attainments might differ significantly, the adjusted attainments would not. We should note, too, that it is the differences among the adjusted attainments which are the more important, for these are the differences that would result if all the groups had been equated for intelligence in the first place. If the adjusted means were found to differ significantly, we could be sure that this was not a consequence of the group differences in intelligence, for these differences—even if they happened to be considerable—have been controlled statistically. Because of this control, we could arrive at much the same result as if the groups had been matched for intelligence in the first place.

9.2 An analysis of covariance

The detailed procedure in an analysis of covariance can be illustrated by an investigation similar to one conducted by Jones *et al.* (1957) into certain educational aspects of English–Welsh bilingualism. Children brought up in Welsh-speaking homes might, it is thought, be less fluent in English even at the end of their primary-school education—the medium of school instruction being English—than monoglot English-speaking children from homes where little or no Welsh is heard. For the purpose of the investigation, children are divided into categories of linguistic background, a possible division being (1) a category of children where Welsh is habitually spoken at home by both parents; (2) a category of children where Welsh is spoken only occasionally at home; and (3) a category of children where Welsh is never spoken at home. Random groups of ten-year-old children are then selected from each category, and each group is given (a) a test of

Table 9.1 Scores of three groups on two tests (for analysis of covariance)

	Groups					
	1		2		3	
	Test X	Test Y	Test X	Test Y	Test X	Test Y
	34	37	39	37	42	41
	38	34	41	42	46	39
	40	37	44	40	48	37
	43	39	48	40	50	42
	46	37	50	46	52	46
	48	41	52	43	53	44
	50	42	54	47	56	48
	51	39	59	45	59	45
	55	40	60	53	60	52
	56	46	65	50	64	48
Sum	461	392	512	443	530	452
Mean	46·1	39·2	51·2	44·3	53·0	45·2

	Test X	Test Y
Overall sum	1503	1287
Overall mean	50·1	42·9

non-verbal intelligence, and (b) a test in the usage of English. Table 9.1 shows sets of test scores for ten children in each group. (In an actual investigation the group numbers would be far larger.) X refers to non-verbal intelligence and Y to English. We see that the group means in both tests differ considerably. The aim is to adjust the differences in English for the differences in intelligence.

We begin by calculating the regression of English (Y) on intelligence (X) for each of the groups separately. To do this, the corrected sum of squares for X and the corrected sum of products XY are needed for each group. (A corrected sum of squares has been explained in section 2.2 as the sum of squares of scores expressed as deviations from their mean; a corrected sum of products is similarly the sum of products of scores, each score being expressed as a deviation from its own group mean.) The calculation of these sums is shown in table 9.2. (The corrected sums of squares for Y have also been calculated, as these will be needed later.) The regression of Y on X is then given by dividing the sum of products by the sum of squares for X, i.e. by $\frac{\sum xy}{\sum x^2}$. This works out at 0·357 for group 1, 0·493 for group 2 and 0·417 for group 3.

Each regression shows the overall extent to which the Y scores increase with X. Consider, for instance, the regression 0·357 for group 1. This is shown by the slope or gradient of the oblique line in figure 8. The points representing the X and Y scores of the ten children are also shown. The regression line, which also passes through the point representing the X and Y mean scores of the group, is such that the vertical (Y) deviations of the points from it are a minimum, i.e. the sum of the deviations above the line equals the sum of the deviations below the line, and the sum of the squares of all the deviations is less than would be the case for any other straight line. The line is a 'best-fitting' in this sense. In the same way, the regressions for groups 2 and 3 are also best-fitting lines for the scores of their group.

A further point is that a sum of squares of the deviations from the regression line—the sum which is a minimum for the particular line—is given for each group by $\sum y^2 - \frac{(\sum xy)^2}{\sum x^2}$. If the regression is based on n scores, this sum will have $(n-2)$ degrees of freedom, not $(n-1)$, since a further degree of freedom is lost by the fixing of the regression line. This sum of squares is shown for the three groups in the first three lines of table 9.3.

Table 9.2 Calculations of sums of squares and products for the groups in table 9.1

(i) *Group 1*

$$\Sigma X = 34+38+\cdots+56 = 461 : \Sigma X^2 = 34^2+38^2+\cdots+56^2 = 21{,}731$$

$$\therefore \text{ Corrected sum of squares, } \Sigma x^2 = 21{,}731 - \frac{461\times 461}{10} = 478{\cdot}9$$

$$\Sigma Y = 37+34+\cdots+46 = 392 : \Sigma Y^2 = 37^2+34^2+\cdots+46^2 = 15{,}466$$

$$\therefore \text{ Corrected sum of squares, } \Sigma y^2 = 15{,}466 - \frac{392\times 392}{10} = 99{\cdot}6$$

$$\Sigma XY = 34.37+38.34+\cdots+56.46 = 18{,}242$$

$$\therefore \text{ Corrected sum of products, } \Sigma xy = 18{,}242 - \frac{461\times 392}{10} = 170{\cdot}8$$

(ii) *Group 2*

$$\Sigma X = 39+41+\cdots+65 = 512 : \Sigma X^2 = 39^2+41^2+\cdots+65^2 = 26{,}868$$

$$\therefore \text{ Corrected sum of squares, } \Sigma x^2 = 26{,}868 - \frac{512\times 512}{10} = 653{\cdot}6$$

$$\Sigma Y = 37+42+\cdots+50 = 443 : \Sigma Y^2 = 37^2+42^2+\cdots+50^2 = 19{,}841$$

$$\therefore \text{ Corrected sum of squares, } \Sigma y^2 = 19{,}841 - \frac{443\times 443}{10} = 216{\cdot}1$$

$$\Sigma XY = 39.37+41.42+\cdots+65.50 = 23{,}004$$

$$\therefore \text{ Corrected sum of products, } \Sigma xy = 23{,}004 - \frac{512\times 443}{10} = 322{\cdot}4$$

(iii) *Group 3*

$$\Sigma X = 42+46+\cdots+64 = 530 : \Sigma X^2 = 42^2+46^2+\cdots+64^2 = 28{,}510$$

$$\therefore \text{ Corrected sum of squares, } \Sigma x^2 = 28{,}510 - \frac{530\times 530}{10} = 420{\cdot}0$$

$$\Sigma Y = 41+39+\cdots+48 = 452 : \Sigma Y^2 = 41^2+39^2+\cdots+48^2 = 20{,}564$$

$$\therefore \text{ Corrected sum of squares, } \Sigma y^2 = 20{,}564 - \frac{452\times 452}{10} = 133{\cdot}6$$

$$\Sigma XY = 42.41+46.39+\cdots+64.48 = 24{,}131$$

$$\therefore \text{ Corrected sum of products, } \Sigma xy = 24{,}131 - \frac{530\times 452}{10} = 175{\cdot}0$$

Note to table 9.2 Just as the corrected sum of squares for X is given by

$$\Sigma x^2 = \Sigma X^2 - \frac{(\Sigma X)^2}{n}$$

and that for Y is given by $\Sigma y^2 = \Sigma Y^2 - \frac{(\Sigma Y)^2}{n}$, so the corrected sum of products is given by a formula of the same mathematical 'shape', i.e.

$$\Sigma xy = \Sigma XY - \frac{(\Sigma X)(\Sigma Y)}{n}$$

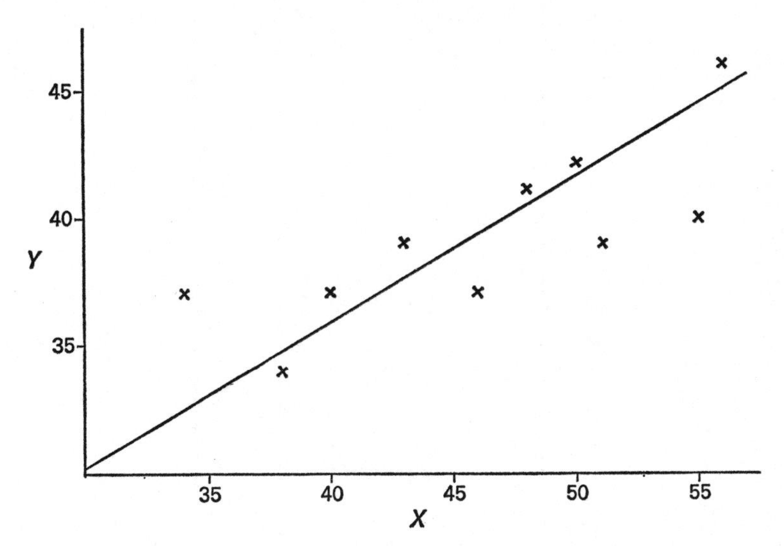

Figure 8 The regression of Y score on X for group 1 in table 9.1

The question of crucial importance is whether the differences among the separate group regressions are statistically significant. If not, the regressions could be averaged, the average regression being the best estimate of the *one* population regression. This average regression would be found by adding together the sum of squares, $\sum x^2$, and the sum of products, $\sum xy$, for the separate groups—these are also shown in the first three lines of table 9.3—and calculating the quotient $\frac{\sum xy}{\sum x^2}$ for these sums. This is shown in line 5 of table 9.3. We see that the average regression comes to

Table 9.3 Analysis of covariance of the data in table 9.1 (variation within groups)

	Deviations from mean					*Deviations from regression*		
Source of variation	*Degrees of freedom*	$\sum x^2$	$\sum xy$	$\sum y^2$	*Regression* $\frac{\sum xy}{\sum x^2}$	*Degrees of freedom*	$\sum y^2 - \frac{(\sum xy)^2}{\sum x^2}$	*Mean square*
Within group 1	9	478·9	170·8	99·6	0·357	8	38·68	4·84
Within group 2	9	653·6	322·4	216·1	0·493	8	56·07	7·01
Within group 3	9	420·0	175·0	133·6	0·417	8	60·68	7·59
						24	155·43	6·48
Within groups (1+2+3)	27	1,552·5	668·2	449·3	0·430	26	161·71	6·22

0·430. The sum of squares of the deviations from this average regression has also been obtained—in precisely the same way as the corresponding sums for the separate regressions. This sum, 161·71, has been obtained from all the scores, and can be compared with 155·43 (line 4 of the table), the sum obtained by adding together the sums for the separate regressions.

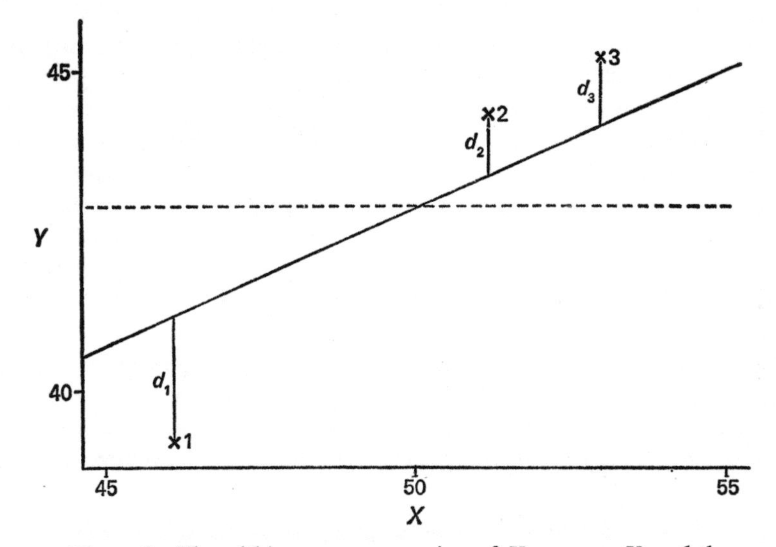

Figure 9 The within-groups regression of *Y* score on *X*, and the mean *X* and *Y* scores of the groups (data from table 9.1). The overall *Y* mean is shown by the horizontal line. Each adjusted group mean is given by overall mean plus the deviation from the regression line (d_1, d_2 or d_3 as shown above).

The former sum is necessarily larger than the latter, since the average regression does not provide the best-fitting line for any of the groups. The difference between the two sums, however, gives a measure of the variation among the group regressions. The difference, which works out as 6·28, has $26-24 = 2$ degrees of freedom (necessarily so, since there are three separate regressions), and the mean square is tested against the mean square from the sum of the separate regressions, 6·48. We see that $F = \frac{3{\cdot}14}{6{\cdot}48} < 1$ so that the differences among the separate group regressions are not significant. It follows that the averaging of the separate regressions *is* legitimate, and one can proceed to adjust the group means for Y on this basis.

Figure 9 shows the X and Y group means in relation to the average regression of Y scores on X, 0·430. The precise extent of the adjustments to the Y means necessary because of the differing X means is now apparent. While differences among the actual Y means are shown by the heights of the points—or their deviations from the horizontal line drawn through the overall mean—adjusting to take account of the X differences brings in the regression line as a new basis for comparison. It is the vertical deviations of the points from the regression line (not the horizontal line) which measure differences among the Y means *adjusted for the differences in X*. We see, for instance, that the points for groups 2 and 3 are about the same distance above the regression line, so the adjusted means for these groups will differ only slightly. The point for group 1, on the other hand, is below the regression line, so that its adjusted mean will be the lowest of the three. (Even so, the differences from the groups 2 and 3 will be considerably less than for the unadjusted means.) The amount of adjustment will be determined by the product of (a) the deviation of the X group mean from the overall X mean, and (b) the regression of Y on X. Table 9.4 records these products for each of the groups, together with the adjusted means.

Table 9.4 Calculation of the adjusted group means (data from table 9.1)

Group	*X mean*	*Deviation from overall mean* (50·1)	*Deviation × regression* (0·430)	*Y mean*	*Adjusted Y mean*
1	46·1	−4·0	−1·72	39·2	39·2−(−1·72) = 40·92
2	51·2	1·1	0·47	44·3	44·3−0·47 = 43·83
3	53·0	2·9	1·25	45·2	45·2−1·25 = 43·95

There remains the question of whether the adjusted means differ significantly. To answer this, it is the deviations from the regression that must be considered, the deviations between groups and within groups. The sum of squares of the deviations within groups has already been obtained (line 5 of table 9.3). The sum for between groups is obtained by subtracting this from the sum of squares of the deviations for the total variation, i.e. the sum for all the scores irrespective of their separation into groups. We begin, then, by calculating the sum of squares of the deviations from the mean for the total variation. This follows the same pattern as that for the separate groups (table 9.2), and is given in table 9.5. The sum of squares of the deviations from the regressions then follows from $\sum y^2 - \frac{(\sum xy)^2}{x^2}$ as before. It is shown on the first line of table 9.6.

The second line of table 9.6 is the within-groups variation previously obtained in table 9.3. The sum of squares of the deviations from regression in this line is subtracted from the sum in the first line to give the sum of squares for between groups, 50·84. The degrees of freedom are also subtracted, giving $28 - 26 = 2$. The mean square for between groups is therefore 25·42. This is tested for significance against the mean square for within groups, giving $F = \frac{25{\cdot}42}{6{\cdot}22} = 4{\cdot}09$, which for 2 and 26 degrees of freedom is significant at the 5-per-cent level (statistical table 2A). We may conclude that there are real group differences in performance in the English test, even after allowance has been made for the group differences in non-verbal intelligence.

The reader will observe that the between-groups sum of squares has been obtained by subtraction, i.e. total sum minus within-groups sum, which is a reversal of the usual procedure. He may wonder, too, why a between-groups sum of squares could not have been calculated directly from the between-groups sums $\sum x^2$, $\sum xy$ and $\sum y^2$, the sums of squares and products of the deviations from the mean. (These—the missing entries of the third line of table 9.6—could easily have been obtained from the group sums $\sum X$ and $\sum Y$ in the usual way. Again, the within-groups sums in line 2 could then have been verified by subtraction from line 1.) The between-groups regression, however, which is what we would then be using, is directly bound up with the differences among the Y means—differences which are being adjusted and then tested for significance—and so the method of adjustment would not be independent of the differences tested.

Table 9.5 Calculation of sums of squares and products for the total variation in table 9.1

$$\sum X = 34+38+ \cdots +64 = 1503 : \sum X^2 = 34^2+38^2+ \cdots +64^2 = 77{,}109$$

$$\therefore \quad \text{Corrected sum of squares, } \sum x^2 = 77{,}109 - \frac{1503 \times 1503}{30} = 1808{\cdot}7$$

$$\sum Y = 37+34+ \cdots +48 = 1287 : \sum y^2 = 37^2+34^2+ \cdots +48^2 = 55{,}871$$

$$\therefore \quad \text{Corrected sum of squares, } \sum y^2 = 55{,}871 - \frac{1287 \times 1287}{30} = 658{\cdot}7$$

$$\sum XY = 34.37+38.34+ \cdots +64.48 = 65{,}377$$

$$\therefore \quad \text{Corrected sum of products, } \sum xy = 65{,}377 - \frac{1503 \times 1287}{30} = 898{\cdot}3$$

Finally, we should be aware that adjusting group means in the manner described could lead to the differences among them being increased. Suppose that in our present illustration a test of comprehension of Welsh had also been given. (We will assume that groups 2 and 3, though hearing relatively little or no Welsh at home, had been learning the language as a school subject.) Group 1, despite its lower intelligence, would almost certainly have the highest attainment in Welsh. If, therefore, the within-groups regression still showed an increase in attainment with intelligence, adjusting for the differences in intelligence would necessarily increase the difference between group 1 and the other groups. The same situation would occur in a methods experiment, if the group with the lowest intelligence had nevertheless secured the highest attainment mean. The full extent of the superiority of the particular method is then brought out only by the adjusted means.

9.3 The model

The model for the experiment described in the last section may be written as

$$y_{ij} = M + A_i + Bx_{ij} + e_{ij}$$

where y_{ij} is the score of person j in group i in the test of English;
M is a component common to all the English scores;
A_i is a component common to all the English scores of group i;
B is the regression of English score on intelligence, common to all the groups;
x_{ij} is the score of person j in group i in the test of intelligence, this score being expressed as a deviation from the overall mean score, i.e. the mean intelligence score of all the groups;
and e_{ij} is a component specific to person j of group i.

In the particular experiment i takes on the values 1, 2 and 3, and j the values from 1 to 10. Comparing the model with that for randomized groups (section 3.3), we see that, apart from the attainment score now being denoted by y_{ij}, the only difference is the introduction of the regression term Bx_{ij}. The four contributions to the score y_{ij} are all independent of each other, and as before e_{ij}—the element of randomness in the design—is such that for any given i it can be regarded as drawn from a normally distributed population with means of zero and a variance

Table 9.6 Analysis of covariance of the data in table 9.1 (variation between and within groups)

	Deviations from mean				*Regression*	*Deviations from regression*		
Source of variation	*Degrees of freedom*	$\sum x^2$	$\sum xy$	$\sum y^2$	$\frac{\sum xy}{\sum x^2}$	*Degrees of freedom*	$\sum y^2 - \frac{(\sum xy)^2}{\sum x^2}$	*Mean square*
Total	29	1,808·7	898·3	658·7		28	212·55	
Within groups	27	1,552·5	668·2	449·3	0·430	26	161·71	6·22
Between groups	2					2	50·84	25·42

of σ^2, which is the same for all the populations, i.e. all values of i in turn.* In the same way, A_i is regarded as being drawn from a normally distributed population with a mean of zero and a variance of σ_A^2. The components analysis then follows the pattern of that for a randomized-groups design (table 3.5), the only difference being 1 degree of freedom less for both the individuals (or within groups) and total sources of variance.

It should be added, too, that, as with the randomized-groups design, there is no necessity for equal numbers of individuals in each group. The model need not assume equal numbers in the groups, and the methods of calculation can easily take account of groups of differing size.

9.4 Basic assumptions

The analysis of covariance exerts a strong attraction for investigators who find it difficult, or inconvenient, to control an extraneous factor experimentally, so it is well to list the assumptions on which the analysis depends. As in the case of other applications of the analysis of variance, these assumptions include normality of distribution and homogeneity of variance (sections 2.3 and 2.6). They also include the assumption mentioned earlier in this chapter, namely that the separate within-groups regressions should differ only by chance. It has also been assumed—though this has not hitherto been stated—that these regressions are linear, i.e. the deviations of the group means from a straight-line fit are themselves chance, so that in particular the means do not follow (or deviate from) a curved regression line.† The basic assumptions may then be listed as follows:

1. The attainment scores Y in each group must be regarded as a random sample from a population of possible scores. The regression of Y on X—the measure forming the basis of the adjustment—is then the same for all these populations. (If this assumption happens to be false, no basis for adjustment exists.)
2. The regression of Y on X, common to all the populations, is linear.

* This assumption was not tested in section 9.2, but the mean squares from the separate groups (recorded in table 9.3) are all estimates of σ^2, and should therefore differ only by chance. Bartlett's test (section 3.6) would confirm that the differences are not significant at the 5-per-cent level.

† See McNemar (1962) for a description of a test for the assumption of linearity of regression.

3. The adjusted scores in each of the populations are normally distributed (the assumption of *normality of distribution*).
4. The adjusted scores in each of the populations have the same variance (the assumption of *homogeneity of variance*).

In addition, if as a result of obtaining statistically significant differences among the adjusted means, we wish to attribute these differences to the differing characteristic of the groups (e.g. to the degree of 'Welshness' of background in the illustration of section 9.2), it is essential that each group be a random sample from a population having the same characteristics. (This assumption is somewhat wider in scope than assumption 1 above.) It is also important that the X measures be unaffected by the group characteristics. Thus, in the illustration of section 9.2 it would be unwise to use scores on a *verbal* intelligence test as the X measures, since these would be affected by 'Welshness' of background. In particular, group 1 who come from homes where little English is spoken would have their test scores artificially depressed, and so an adjustment for intelligence would result in over-compensation. (In a methods experiment, on the other hand, where scores on an intelligence test or an attainment test given before the beginning of the experiment are used as the basis for adjustment, this requirement would obviously be satisfied.) We may, therefore, add to the four assumptions stated above the following:

5. The persons tested in each group constitute a random sample of a population defined by the characteristics of the group (or, at any rate, by the particular characteristics under investigation).
6. The X measures are unaffected by the group characteristics.

9.5 Further considerations

The covariance design has been presented as similar to a randomized-groups design, except that scores on an additional factor are secured for all persons tested. As we have seen, the design then achieves much the same purpose as a randomized-blocks design, the additional factor being controlled statistically not experimentally. There is no reason, however, why an analysis of covariance could not be used in conjunction with a randomized-groups or factorial design, or again with a Latin-square design, provided that scores on an additional factor are secured for all the persons tested, and that all the basic assumptions as set out in the previous section are satisfied. The appropriate model would be the same as for the design when an analysis of covariance is not used apart from an additional term, a term similar to Bx_{ij} in the model of section 9.3. Examples of these designs are given by Federer (1955) and Snedecor (1956).

The principle of controlling an extraneous factor statistically by an analysis of covariance could be extended to more than one factor. Adjustments would then be made by means of the multiple regression of the (criterion) attainment scores on the extraneous factors controlled. Thus, in comparing the attainments of randomized groups we could control both intelligence and attainment on a suitable pre-test. The advantage gained—judged by the reduction in the mean square for error—would depend upon the magnitude of the multiple correlation compared with that of the single correlation between the final attainment and either intelligence or the initial attainment, whichever is the higher. Experience in the educational field has shown that the multiple correlation is often not very much higher than the highest of the two or more correlations between the criterion and the separate measures—always provided that the measures already selected for possible statistical control are among the most suitable. (There would, of course, be no point in controlling a measure that had a near-zero correlation with the criterion if other measures were readily available.) The advantage gained by simultaneously controlling more than one measure would then be only slight.* Another possibility would be that combining the two or more extraneous factors into a single composite measure at the outset (see, for example, Dunnette and Hoggatt 1957).

In conclusion, some further comparisons between the covariance and randomized-blocks design may be helpful. With randomized blocks the controlled measure is used only to form the groups; it plays no further part in the analysis. The measures, too, must be known at the beginning of the experiment. With analysis of covariance, on the other hand, the controlled measures form the basis of the entire analysis. They could be secured, however, either during the experiment itself (e.g. the length of time needed to complete a task) or even afterwards (e.g. scores on an intelligence test).

With randomized blocks, an interaction between the treatments and the controlled measure may prove to be of particular importance—more

* If R is the multiple correlation and r the correlation for a single controlled measure, the extent of the advantage will depend upon how much $\sqrt{1-R^2}$ is less than $\sqrt{1-r^2}$.

important possibly than the main effect of the treatments themselves. An interaction does not reveal itself directly in a covariance design, though the assumption of a common (population) regression is substantially equivalent to one of there being no interaction.

This leads us on to noting that the assumptions of the analysis of covariance are the more restrictive. Randomized blocks require only normality of distribution and homogeneity of variance. In particular, no assumption as to the nature of the regression is required. We may conclude, then, that the analysis of covariance should be preferred only when practical considerations militate against the use of randomized blocks, and when confidence is justified that its more restrictive assumptions are satisfied.

References

DUNNETTE, M. D. and HOGGATT, A. C. (1957) 'Deriving a composite score from several measures of the same attribute,' *Educational and Psychological Measurement*, **17**, 423–34.

FEDERER, W. T. (1955) *Experimental Design*, New York: Macmillan, pp. 487–95.

JONES, W. R., MORRISON, J., ROGERS, J. and SAER, H. (1957) *The Educational Attainment of Bilingual Children in relation to their Intelligence and Linguistic Background*, Cardiff: University of Wales Press.

MCNEMAR, Q. (1962) *Psychological Statistics*, New York: Wiley (3rd edition), pp. 272–81.

SNEDECOR, G. W. (1956) *Statistical Methods*, Iowa State College Press (5th edition), pp. 404–12.

Index

Page numbers in *italics* refer to works cited in the references.

(Index by G. Dixon)

Acknowledgments

The author and publishers are indebted to the Literary Executor of the late Sir Ronald A. Fisher, F.R.S., Cambridge, to Dr Frank Yates, F.R.S., Rothamsted, and to Messrs Oliver & Boyd Ltd, Edinburgh, for permission to reprint adaptations of tables 3, 4 and 5 from their book *Statistical Tables for Biological, Agricultural and Medical Research*; to Houghton Mifflin Company for permission to reprint tables 4 and 5 from E. F. Lindquist's *Design and Analysis of Experiments in Psychology and Education*; and to Dr C. A. Boneau and the *Psychological Bulletin* for permission to reprint the table originally printed in *Psychological Bulletin*, **57**, 1, 1960.